No Place Like Home

Fishing and Hunting
Adventures Across Canada

KEN BAILEY

Foreword by Jim Shockey

The Publisher: OverTime Books is an imprint of Éditions de la Montagne Verte

Library and Archives Canada Cataloguing in Publication

Title: No place like home : fishing and hunting adventures across Canada / Ken Bailey.
Other titles: fishing and hunting adventures across Canada
Names: Bailey, Ken, 1958– author.
Identifiers: Canadiana (print) 20190137983 | Canadiana (ebook) 20190140828 | ISBN 9781897277942 (softcover) |
 ISBN 9781897277959 (EPUB)
Subjects: LCSH: Bailey, Ken, 1958-—Anecdotes. | LCSH: Fishing—Canada—Anecdotes. |LCSH: Hunting—Canada—Anecdotes.
Classification: LCC SK35 .B35 2019 | DDC 799/.0971—dc23

Project Director: Deanna Moeller
Illustrations: Jane Bailey
Cover Image: arianstevens / Getty Images

We acknowledge the financial support of the Government of Canada. Nous reconnaissons l'appui financier du gouvernement du Canada.

Funded by the Government of Canada
Financé par le gouvernement du Canada | Canadä

PC: 39

Contents

Dedication

To all those with whom I've shared a tent,
a boat, a cabin, a blind, a streambank or a campfire.
You know who you are. Thank you. I enjoyed every minute
and learned from each and every one of you.

Acknowledgements

Many to whom I owe a debt of gratitude are named in the pages of this book. Your friendship means the world to me, and I'll never be able to repay what you've given me.

My sincere thanks are also extended to the many editors who willingly provided me space in their magazines; without your generosity, many of the adventures described in these pages would not have been possible. In particular, I would like to acknowledge Patrick Walsh, my long-time editor at *Outdoor Canada*. I truly appreciate the support, guidance and freedom you've given me over many years. Hopefully we have a few stories yet to tell together.

As I read through the adventures recounted in these pages, it dawns on me that the person with whom I've spent more days afield than any other doesn't appear. Rollie Beisswenger and I have shared a hunting camp for almost three decades and have spent countless days together with rod or gun in hand. My thanks to Rollie for being such a great partner.

I leaned on an old friend, Jim Shockey, to write the foreword to this book. When we first met, he was just beginning his career as an outfitter and outdoors communicator. Today he is arguably the most well-known and respected hunter and advocate for the hunting community on the planet. I sincerely appreciate that he made time in his busy schedule to contribute to this project, and the fact that he did tells you everything you need to know about the man.

My appreciation is extended, too, to Faye Boer, Sonnet Press and Deanna Moeller, OverTime Books, who believed in my writing and did their best against significant odds to make my efforts presentable.

Lastly, but most importantly, I want to thank my wife, Jane, for her continued love, support and friendship while I was gallivanting around. I'm thankful every day that she has questionable taste in men! It's Jane's line art that graces the pages of this book, and I am forever grateful that I've had the opportunity to watch the magic that appears whenever she touches paint or ink to paper. As always, I look a whole lot better because of her.

Foreword

Thanks to renowned troubadour Stompin' Tom Connors, Canada already has an iconic song about this amazing land, arguably several, but we have not had an iconic book about the wonders of Canada's hunting and fishing opportunities. A book that takes us on a journey from one side of this land to the other, sharing the beauty of Ungava Bay or the solitude of the mighty Muskwa River in BC, or the spectacular isolation of the Barren Lands to the north and the Acadian rhythm to the east. No iconic book that takes us hunting and fishing on Vancouver Island and to the George River and to so many other spectacular places within our borders…until now.

Not taking anything away from Stompin' Tom, but speaking as both a humble singer/songwriter ("Howl With Me") and published scribe, my opinion is that it's much easier to write lyrics and music celebrating the joys of our "home and native land" than it is to write a book about this nearly indescribably wondrous thing we call the Canadian outdoors.

We have a song(s), yes, because that's easy! The very essence of music lends itself to "feeling," in a way that words never can—"The fourth, the fifth, the minor fall and the major lift." As you soar with the chords, it's difficult not to feel and share in the enlightened vision of "Hallelujah," although granted, the late, great lyrical genius and fellow Canadian, Leonard Cohen, might disagree.

Fair enough. Mr. Cohen would certainly know whereof he speaks. But with a song, at least you have the "music" to fall back on where the artistic command of mere words may fail.

The point being, shouldering the task of using words and words alone to tell the story of the Canadian outdoor experience as it relates to hunting and fishing is a daunting task, a task that only the homegrown Canadian scribbling equivalent of a Stompin' Tom or a Leonard Cohen could have ever accomplished.

Enter Ken Bailey.

We go back a long, long way…three decades long if memory serves. We were both "writers" back then, although granted, one of us (who recognized their talent lay elsewhere), became an outfitter and television host, while the other stayed the course, honing, constantly honing, his craft. One of us left Canada over and over again, travelling 300-plus days per year up, down and around this lovely green planet for more than 30 years, while the other explored intimately this place we call Canada.

Yep. I was the peregrinator lacking in writing talent, which explains why I am not the one with my name on the title page of this iconic book on the Canadian outdoor hunting and fishing experience. And yep (which I don't even believe is a word in the Queen's English), it was Ken Bailey who devoted his life to experiencing and writing about "inner" Canada.

Yep, it was Ken Bailey who penned this entire book worth of the perfectly chosen words to describe the feelings that we, who love nature; that we, who love this land called

Canada; and that we, who hunt and fish, were not gifted with the literary eloquence to actually write ourselves.

Yep, it was Ken Bailey who wrote what we all feel…*No Place Like Home.*

Nobody else could have accomplished this. No other Canadian outdoor writer is so amply qualified in every regard. No other Canadian outdoor writer has the combination of experience, wisdom and word-wise eloquence to create the iconic work that is *No Place Like Home.*

Thank you Ken. On behalf of all the rest of us, thank you for being our champion!

Also Ken, thank you for allowing me to dust off the old typewriting skills to put to words how I feel about your book, something that in a reverse negative kind of way I am amply qualified to do! For all the travelling I've done since we first met all those years ago, all the years I've spent on the road, have made me somewhat of an expert on how amazing our home and native land is!

Trust me.

For the hunter and the fisherman, there really is no place like home.

–Jim Shockey, hunter,
conservationist, television personality
and outdoors communicator

Introduction

I was a lucky kid. Throughout my younger years, I had no doubt about how I would one day make my living. A passion for wildlife and wild places seemed to come naturally to me; I was one of those kids who regularly came home with snakes, frogs or bits of eggshell in my pocket. In those early days I idolized Marlin Perkins and Jacques Cousteau, hosts of the only wildlife programs on television at the time. It seemed like they were enjoying pretty good lives, travelling from one exotic location to another as they explored our natural world.

I was also a service brat, the son of a Canadian Air Force pilot. We moved often, as is common for military families, so I saw a lot of Canada as a kid. In fact, I attended eight different schools before completing high school. Wherever you were from, I was from there, too. While it was difficult to leave friends, I clearly had an explorer's blood in me as I was always eager to discover the natural wonders of wherever we were going next.

When I was old enough, fishing and hunting became part of my exploration. I fondly recall as a 10-year-old, fishing many summer days from the government dock in Belleville on Ontario's Moira River. A couple of years later we began riding our bicycles 10 miles to a friend's farm, where we'd plink away at woodchucks with a couple of rusty Cooey .22s. But it was upon our move to Winnipeg, when I was 15, that my passion for hunting really flourished. My father had hung up his rifles and rods when I was quite young, so what I really needed was a mentor. As luck would have it, I found one in a new high school friend, Brian Hagglund, and his father, Howard. The Hagglunds were avid waterfowlers and graciously invited me along on hunts and family trap shoots. I couldn't hit a blessed thing to begin with, but they were considerate and patient enough to teach me the basics, and eventually, it got so that I could knock down the occasional unlucky duck or goose.

Fast forward a half dozen years, and I was a college graduate with a crisp diploma in fisheries and wildlife management in one hand and a suitcase in the other, eager to begin a professional life as the next Cousteau. I quickly discovered, however, it doesn't exactly work that way, and I was relegated to taking whatever short-term contract work I could find. I tracked inconnu, a large whitefish, fitted with radio transmitters in the NWT's Slave River; conducted bird surveys along Alberta's Athabasca River; measured deer jaws collected from hunters; banded geese; surveyed elk habitat use as it related to pipeline construction; counted sharp-tailed grouse dancing grounds—in short, whatever project I could find that padded my resumé and paid enough to cover the rent. Eventually, I landed a full-time position with Ducks Unlimited, and that stability allowed me to resume hunting and fishing on a more regular basis.

Life never unfolds along the straight line you envision. It was a chance meeting with a Ducks Unlimited volunteer, Kevin Rolfe, that launched my writing efforts. Kevin published an annual magazine, *Rolfe's Alberta Hunting Guide*, and after meeting him at a youth mentoring event, he asked me to write a duck hunting article. That first article led, a couple of years later, to me leaving Ducks Unlimited and joining Kevin full-time. Over the ensuing few years, we expanded to printing five annuals and one bimonthly magazine, *The Outdoor Edge.* I served as editor while Kevin handled the advertising and design. I didn't really know the first thing about editing a magazine, but learned as I went along.

On the advice of Bruce Masterman, who was then the outdoors columnist for the *Calgary Herald,* I joined the Outdoor Writers of Canada (OWC) as a means to more fully engage in the outdoor writing community. That membership led to another chance encounter that would eventually help shape my writing life. I didn't know a soul when I attended my first OWC annual convention in 1990. So when I climbed onto a bus that was taking attendees to a breakout session where we'd shoot rifles, tie flies and generally do outdoor "stuff," I grabbed the first unoccupied seat I found. Sitting next to me was a woman in her late 50s who I soon learned was Teddi Brown, the editor of *Outdoor Canada.* Teddi and her publication were icons, representing the very pinnacle of Canada's outdoor writing industry. She was a Lou Grant type, a little gruff, with every word carefully measured. Over the course of that bus ride, we chatted about outdoor writing, with me hanging on her every word.

Three years later, I sold my interest in the magazine and returned to the wildlife field. I'd barely gotten settled into my new life when the phone rang. It was Teddi, wondering whether I'd be interested in writing *Outdoor Canada's* wildlife column. Would I? I'd hoped to stay active as a freelance writer, and this was an opportunity too good to be true. That was in 1994. Two years later, when the magazine's editorial profile changed, I began writing the hunting column, and continue to do so today.

I have remained active in the wildlife and habitat con-servation field, assuming a number of roles as an employee before starting my own consulting business. I never did grow to be the second coming of Jacques Cousteau.

I've continued to be an active freelance outdoors writer, as a columnist for *Outdoor Canada* and as a contribu-tor to a handful of other publications both in Canada and beyond. Having access to the media opened up a world of opportunities for me, including invitations to hunt and fish in places I would never have otherwise visited. Over the years, I've traversed parts of South America, Europe and Africa with rod or gun in hand. More rewarding has been the chance to explore nearly every nook and cranny of Canada. It is those adventures that form the basis for this book.

Canadians are blessed to live in a country with a nearly unrivalled diversity of landscapes. That diversity translates into a broad array of habitat types, along with the fish and wildlife populations they support. From the Arctic's barren grounds to the vast southern prairies, from the dark boreal forest to the rocky coastlines, and from roaring rivers to clear, cold lakes, I've treasured the opportunities to experience Canada from a sportsman's perspective.

No Place Like Home celebrates Canada's sporting opportunities and lifestyle—a throwback to a time when stories about our great outdoors were meant to entertain, unlike much of the modern sporting press that focuses on the "how-to" or "where-to." If you learn anything here, please accept my apologies, it's purely by accident! What you will find instead are first-hand accounts of my adventures hunting and fishing from coast to coast to coast. Some have been previously published in similar versions in magazines, while others are printed here for the first time. You may note that I use both metric and imperial measurements in these stories. I've tried to select between them in a manner that is consistent with how Canadian outdoorsmen and women use them. If I've offended any grammar gurus, maybe you should go fishing or hunting more often. You need to relax a little.

My hope is that when you read these stories, sitting by a crackling fire on a cold winter's evening, your favourite beverage at hand, you'll be reminded of adventures of your own, or inspired to fish or hunt a region of Canada you've not yet visited. One should never undervalue how much of life's richness exists in memory and anticipation.

–Ken Bailey

1

CONFESSIONS OF
A GEORGE RIVER JUNKIE

Atlantic salmon are acknowledged as the pinnacle of Canadian fish to target on a fly. Previous to this trip with Sammy Cantafio, I'd fished Atlantic salmon only once, and had no success. That seems to be par for the course with these quintessential fish. Or so I thought. Sammy and the George River taught me that in the right place, at the right time, with the right mentorship, Atlantic salmon can be more fact than artifact. For those who've never had the opportunity to fish with Sammy at their side, you've unfortunately missed your opportunity because he no longer operates on the George River.

You can do everything absolutely right in a battle with an Atlantic salmon and still come out second best. While that may not seem particularly fair, it's the uncertainty, the utter lack of assuredness every time you hook into one, that gives this salmon its legendary status within angling circles.

Of course, it doesn't exactly boost your confidence, especially after it's already been knocked to the rocks a few times, hearing your guide chant, "Back to the kiddie's pool for you!" And this after you've failed, yet again, to tame 15 pounds of raw flesh and will. But I knew what the deal was when I ventured to Helen's Falls Salmon Camp in northern Québec's remote Ungava Peninsula.

After all, the invitation from outfitter Sammy Cantafio had come with its own special brand of admonishment. He'd made it clear he was going to teach me how to fish Atlantic salmon on the famed George River, but that I was going to have to be willing to listen and learn. These fish, he warned, have a way of unceremoniously dismissing the uninitiated or unskilled. His words were prophetic, as I was soon to discover.

Following a 20-minute boat ride upstream, we beached below Pool 1, the aptly named first of a dozen or so pools over one of the most gorgeous stretches of wilderness river you could ever hope to wade. For three kilometres, a series of ledges, falls and chutes collectively form the first major obstacle for Atlantic salmon on their way upstream from the saltwater of the Hudson Strait to their spawning beds on the upper George.

Before turning me loose on the pool, Sammy gave me a series of instructions, beginning and ending with, "Wait until you actually see or feel a salmon take your fly before you set the hook." About 10 minutes later, a silver form rose from the dark, deep water below my fly as it skittered across the current. I set the hook…before I saw or felt the fish take my fly.

There it was, lesson number one, shot to hell already. I groaned at my rookie mistake. Sammy just shook his head in equal parts amusement and feigned disgust, and I went back to casting. Three hours of instruction, repeated casting and no fish later, it was time to head back to camp for supper.

After dinner, Sammy and I talked fishing until the wee hours. There was only one other serious angler in camp, a teacher from Vermont who was enjoying his 24th consecutive year fishing the George, but he'd hit the hay early. So over a couple of hours and a couple of sundowners, Sammy talked about his life in the North, of Atlantic salmon and of his passion for fishing, all the while imparting little nuggets of information that would turn out to be of immense value in the coming days on the water.

I first met Sammy a few years earlier when he invited me up for an Ungava caribou hunt. Over the week I spent in pursuit of big bulls, as well as world-class brook trout, I learned what many others had long before discovered— Sammy's operations are top-drawer, from his camps and guides to the game and fish populations that inhabit this area in Québec's northernmost extremes.

A lifelong hunting and fishing addict, Sammy started his career in sales, a vocation that serves him well to this day. He has a unique way of making you feel good, even when he's dressing you down, as I learned first-hand every time another silvery beauty escaped back into its pool. A yearning for adventure soon led him down a different career path; however, and he qualified first as a private pilot then as a commercial pilot and instructor.

Eventually tiring of flying full-time, Sammy followed his nose north and settled in Kuujjuaq, a small community on the Koksoak River just south of Ungava Bay. By then, all the ingredients were in place—a love of the outdoors, a pilot's licence, connections in the North and a knack for salesmanship. And, oh yeah, he's a professional fly tier to boot. Life as an outfitter was all but inevitable at that point, and Sammy has been living both the romance and the adversity of the profession ever since.

The next morning after breakfast, Sammy introduced me to Nathan Wellman, a young man who would be my guide for the rest of my six-day stay. Sammy's angling advice must have sunk in during my hours of slumber because I began the day with two salmon hooked, played and landed before 9:00 AM. Although neither was particularly large—one about eight pounds, the other a pound or so less—they were honest-to-God Atlantic salmon. And I was no longer a salmon virgin.

Over the years, I've read plenty on fly fishing for Atlantic salmon, and these fish performed as advertised, rising suddenly and spectacularly, stretching to the sky before throwing off soul-stirring plumes of water as they crashed back down.

The river was unusually high during my visit, adding an extra challenge. Some of the best pools disappear altogether in high water, and the salmon move through much more quickly than normal, unencumbered by the usual chicane of rocks and ledges. As a result, we skipped straight from Pool 2, where I'd landed the second fish, up to Pool 5½.

It was slow going. The George's shoreline reminded me of pictures I've seen of Mount Everest's base camp, with broad sheets of angled granite pocked by a veritable minefield of ankle-destroying boulders. It was made all the more treacherous by a steady drizzle, and I skidded and danced my way over and around the rocks like a bear on skates.

When we eventually arrived at Pool 5½, I hadn't made 10 downstream and across casts when the water around my #6 Green Monster erupted, and I had another fish on. I was just beginning to figure I had this whole salmon game sussed when the fish, a beautiful 12-pounder, cleared the water, shook its head and spit the hook at me in clear disdain.

I turned to Sammy, eyes lowered, waiting for what I knew was coming. "Lower your rod, and bow to the fish when it jumps, Ken," he scolded. "Remember what we talked about!" Although I'd had little previous Atlantic salmon experience—just two fishless days on the famous Miramichi—I'm no rookie angler. And since I know how to play a fish, I could only agree with Sammy's assessment and chastise myself accordingly for mistakes I knew better than to make.

As it turned out, the rest of the day was fishless—a few followed, some rolled under the fly and others just refused at the last second. As I was learning, this was typical behaviour for Atlantic salmon, fish as renowned for being as picky about what they eat as the most highly paid supermodels.

The next morning greeted us with cool, nervous weather, the clouds clinging to the valley walls and dropping a steady mist of rain that didn't let up all day. Nathan, Sammy and I jumped into the boat for the by now familiar short run upstream. The George is a broad, brawling river, with a strong current that was only strengthening as the water continued to rise. It was now some four or five feet higher than the norm, and we were losing accessible pools by the day.

Despite the George's tumultuous personality, Nathan guided the boat upstream with the assurance of someone who's lived on the water his whole life. Not surprising, considering he, like most of Sammy's guides, grew up in a small fishing community on the remote north shore of the St. Lawrence. Nathan's father is a lobsterman, and when Nathan isn't guiding, he's at home pulling traps, setting nets and generally making his living on a boat.

Sammy's guides are not the type you'll see gracing the cover of a fishing catalogue, decked out in the latest fishing fashions. No, the standard guide's uniform at Helen's Falls consists of blue jeans, work shirts, rubber boots and yellow rain slickers. But as I quickly discovered, what these guys may lose in style points, they more than make up for in hard work, know-how on the water and a true passion for fishing. These fellows have fish tattooed on their souls, the kind of guides you can only hope to get when you step out of a float plane onto the shores of a remote lake or river. They all speak with what I would loosely describe as a Newfoundland accent, and although I couldn't always understand perfectly what Nathan was saying, I always knew exactly what he meant.

The morning's fishing treated me exactly as the weather did, with little sympathy. In the first two hours I hooked and subsequently lost three fish, including one that would have approached the 20-pound class, a true trophy salmon for this river. Unlike some of the more famous New Brunswick and Québec rivers, where 30-pound-plus Atlantics are hooked every year, 25 pounds is about the largest you can expect on the George, with anything more than 15 considered a "really nice fish."

The first two salmon broke off my leader on the jagged rocks that litter the riverbed, while the third, the biggest, jumped across the pool and slid down a chute and over a ledge before I could react. When I did attempt to deal with the situation, I simply clamped down on my reel and, naturally, broke the leader. In hindsight, if I'd just let him go down to the pool below, I could have scrambled down the rocks and fought him from there. Another rookie mistake.

With every hooked and lost fish, Sammy and Nathan were only stepping up their good-natured jibes. "Back to the kiddie's pool!" "My two-year-old could have landed that one!" "Back to the training wheels for you!" That last taunt was a reference to salmon flies with two hooks to help ensure you stay connected to a fish as it leaps and thrashes. After the previous day, my confidence was soaring, but now it was back on the rocks as I struggled to understand why I was having such dismal results. I was learning my salmon lessons, I guess, the only way one can, through trial, error and heartbreak.

I was also starting to understand the addictive nature of Atlantic salmon angling. This is fishing with a clear and distinct purpose. Every cast must be precise, every swing of the fly followed with clear-eyed intensity. And when you hook an Atlantic, it's an experience unlike any other, a feeling that everything else in your world can, and should, be put on hold.

My biggest tactical error, I was beginning to realize, was that I was playing these fish, not fighting them. There's simply no room for the timid or lackadaisical here. You're battling a fish that is tough, willful and game to the core, fighting as though it has absolutely nothing to lose.

Compounding what the fish themselves bring to the table, everything on the George takes place in relatively cramped quarters. The fish-holding lies are about the size of your dinner table, and the pools where they're found are likely to be no bigger than your combined dining room and living room. You have to keep any salmon you hook in that pool, too; if they get out, they're gone forever. And, of course, you can't let them swim around, or under, any of the refrigerator-sized boulders scattered throughout the pool, or they'll break you off.

They'll also break off if you don't give them just the right amount of slack when they leap, and believe me, they all leap. If you don't turn their heads back when they start swimming away, they'll spit the hook. And even when you do everything right, there's still about a 50-50 chance they'll somehow escape. Truly wild creatures have instincts for survival that most of us will never understand. It's because of all that, I was learning, that angling for Atlantic salmon fishing is unlike any other kind of fishing.

In the world of Atlantic salmon, the George River is one of the most coveted destinations. Consider Rick Yeiser, the teacher from Vermont. He fishes three solid weeks every year: one week for brown trout in Argentina, another for steelhead on Alaska's Kodiak Island and a week on the George for Atlantic salmon. He's fished virtually every famous Atlantic salmon river on the planet, but he's returned to the George every year for almost a quarter-century. When I asked him why, he said there's simply no other river that consistently produces as many Atlantics under such exciting and challenging conditions. Coming from an angler with his credentials, I'd say there's no higher praise for the river.

While I was beginning to feel the stirrings of my own growing addiction, the fish were pretty much "owning" me, as my boys would describe it, not the other way around. Shore lunch provided a much-needed respite from my series of lost fish on that third morning, then it was back into the water at Pool 6. In no time I hooked and landed a fish, not a very big one to be sure, but it was just the confidence booster I needed.

We then ambled back down to Pool 5½, and I worked the water methodically for an hour with nothing to show for my efforts but a tired arm.

"Two more casts, Ken," Nathan eventually hollered from shore.

I edged out a little farther into the swirling water and cast again, with the lie I was trying to reach at the outer limits of my casting ability. Bingo! My fly disappeared in a swirl, and I was into a salmon.

Feeling the resistance of my line, the fish surged skyward, revealing its broad flanks. This one would go 15 pounds for sure, I thought, and I made every effort to remember all I'd learned as the salmon tore back and forth across the pool. Each time it made a run for the life-saving turbulence of the main current, I leaned back on my rod until I was sure something—the rod, the line or the fish—would break. And each time the salmon would give a little, then slash its way back to the pool's centre. I was fighting this fish, not playing it. And I was winning. Twenty minutes after the battle started, Nathan slid the big net under the salmon.

It was a great way to end the day, so we jubilantly headed back to Pool 1, where we had beached the boat earlier. Along the way we came to Pool 2, which had previously bested me that very morning. Nathan suggested we give it a quick try; supper could always wait a few minutes. So I tied on Sammy's favourite fly, a #8 Green Cross, and started to work the water.

Cast, swing, retrieve. Cast, swing, retrieve. It was on about my 10th cast that I saw a dark-backed salmon rise up under my drifting fly before engulfing it. As before, I patiently but firmly worked the fish, feeling more in control than I'd been yet. Eventually, it too succumbed, and as we motored back to camp and the warmth and good food that awaited, I reflected on the highs and lows of my day—seven Atlantic salmon hooked, four landed. All in all, I wouldn't have wanted it to unfold any other way.

The last couple of days in camp were a little more varied. I saw more of the George, with Nathan and Sammy taking me to some of their favourite hot spots, and I fished for brookies and lakers. While I thoroughly enjoyed fishing for them, especially the beautifully hued brook trout, I couldn't get my mind away from thoughts of Atlantic salmon. Even a side trip up the Ford River, a tributary of the George, to check if the Arctic char run had started couldn't pry my thoughts from Helen's Falls, the pools and the salmon.

My final day in camp allowed for only a few hours of fishing, but I was at least able to again feed my newfound addiction by landing the only two salmon I hooked. Sadly, the Twin Otter eventually touched down, and there was little to say or do but shake hands, express my gratitude and keep a stiff upper lip as I climbed aboard. As the plane pulled sharply off the gravel airstrip, I slouched back in my seat, reflecting on what I'd learned. Finally, I understood the allure of the Atlantic salmon.

And while the future of this wonderful fish across much of its home waters remains precarious, the George River had allowed me, if only for a few days, to gain a deeper understanding of the tradition and lore of salmon angling. More than anything, though, I discovered that this type of fishing is not for the mere lucky. It's for those who persevere, exhibit patience and are willing to hone their skills to the highest levels. It's for those who can finally and fully understand that when they go Atlantic salmon fishing, it's not really the fish they're after.

—⁓—

2

WATERFOWLING'S FINAL FRONTIER

I first met Dave Kay in the early 1990s when we both worked for Ducks Unlimited Canada. He's one of those perpetually relaxed and easy-to-be-around people that can keep you entertained for hours, relating the adventures he's experienced in Canada's wild places, particularly from his days in the Arctic. Over the years, we've spent many days together hunting and fishing in some of the most pristine landscapes imaginable. This story of our experience on the NWT's Stagg River describes the first extended trip we took together.

A paid-in-full insurance policy is considered a "must have" whenever heading afield with Dave Kay. A big man with a disproportionately large appetite for wilderness, Dave defines "adventure" just a little differently than the rest of us. I suppose that's not entirely unexpected for someone who spent the best part of a decade working as a waterfowl research biologist in some of the most rugged and remote wilderness in Canada's Arctic, but it goes beyond that. On one outing off the south shore of Baffin Island, Dave awoke from a sound sleep to see his research assistant and tent mate grappling with a shotgun. In a New York second, Dave assessed the situation, grabbed the smoothbore and emptied the magazine into the skull of the polar bear that was halfway through the tent flap, intent on making the two biologists a midnight snack. The bear dropped dead. Inside the tent.

A year later, to the very day, Dave and his research team were in the same area, again searching small remote islands for evidence of nesting eider ducks. What should have been a 10-minute task quickly became a life-threatening ordeal when the dog, brought along on the trip ostensibly to provide a new and effective early warning system against marauding polar bears, chewed through the boat's tether rope, thereby setting their craft adrift in the Arctic's frigid waters. It was three and a half days later before Dave and his four fellow castaways were rescued. Wearing nothing more than light shirts and jeans, and equipped with what little they could find in their pockets, they made it through the harrowing ordeal by living off raw eider eggs and rainwater, and stuffing their clothes with eiderdown from the nests in an attempt to persevere in the subzero nighttime temperatures.

To this day, Dave shrugs off both incidents as little more than minor glitches in a couple of otherwise relatively smooth field seasons. His idea of what constitutes adventure seems to be a complete 180 from how most of us define the term, so it was with more than a little trepidation that I accepted his offer to spend a few days with him at his remote duck camp on Great Slave Lake.

Great Slave Lake would seldom, if ever, come up in a campfire discussion about Canada's top waterfowling locations. Long Point, Lake St. Clair, the prairie potholes, the St. Lawrence River and the coastal tidal marshes are never overlooked, and if the north makes the grade at all, the talk tends to focus on the renowned goose hunting of James Bay. But Great Slave? Its sporting claim to fame rests solely on the broad backs of the lake trout, Arctic grayling and northern pike that ply her ice-water depths. A veritable inland sea encompassing in excess of 44,000 square kilometres, with a bottom that stretches the tape to a mind-numbing depth of 600 metres in some places, Great Slave has certainly earned its world-class reputation as an outstanding fishery. But as is so often the case with such a vast and unique place, those who live close and who really know it well have discovered treasure chests of unmined nuggets, jewels that have escaped the attention of those who are attracted by the more garish and obvious. In the case of Great Slave Lake and its waterfowl, that unpolished gem is the relatively unknown North Arm.

In stark contrast to the greatest part of this huge water body, the North Arm is relatively shallow and turbid. Where a ready supply of incoming freshwater is available and where islands protect shallow bays from the prevailing winds, increased water clarity and temperatures provide ideal conditions for the establishment and growth of aquatic vegetation. In turn, this vegetation offers ideal forage for moulting and migrating waterfowl. Among the best of these locales within the North Arm is that area where the Stagg River enters the lake, some 80 kilometres northwest of Yellowknife. Each fall, thousands of ducks amass in preparation for their long annual sojourn to more southern climes and the rich food resources of their wintering grounds. Within the dense vegetation of the inner marsh at the mouth of the Stagg, mallards, Northern pintails and American wigeon predominate. In the outer marsh, where small, bleak, granite islands rise from the water like clusters of surfacing turtles, the diving ducks hold court. In particular, scaup, ring-necked ducks, goldeneyes and bufflehead, all decked out in their contrasting uniforms of black and white, ply the transition waters between the shallow bays and the open water of the North Arm like rocket-propelled sentries. It was the opportunity to hunt these diving ducks that led me to accept Dave's invitation, potentially risking my hide in doing so if Dave's colourful past held true to form.

Dave and his ever-present companion, Brutus, were there to greet me upon my arrival at the Yellowknife airport. Brutus is a mountain of a Chesapeake Bay retriever, true in stature to the breed's origins that saw it employed as both a working dog and a guard dog on the Atlantic seaboard during the heyday of the market-hunting era. In Brutus' case, however, his size belies his temperament, which is much more in keeping with the sweet nature suggested by the thick, dark honey-coloured coat. A quick trip to the grocery to stock up on food and we were off, the 80-kilometre trip to the Stagg offering a beautiful introduction to the area, resplendent in its fall colours of lemon, apricot and the deepest of greens.

Upon arrival at the Stagg, we quickly loaded Dave's 17-foot Mad Trapper canoe with decoys, food, clothes, waders, sleeping bags, shotguns and ammunition. Not to mention two men and a dog, all of whom exceed their respective breed standard for size. It was a tribute to the canoe manufacturer that we didn't sink like a stone before so much as dipping the first paddle, but in no time we were on our way, our overloaded vessel more reminiscent of a Vancouver harbour scow than anything a self-respecting voyageur would be seen in. The early stages of the paddle were relaxed and inviting, the river current merrily helping us along. As we hit the river mouth, however, a two-metre tall wall of equisetum greeted us, the dog-hair dense horsetail reeds making the swinging of our paddles all but impossible. Out we jumped, our leisurely paddle turned instantly into a veritable death march. I quickly became convinced that either Dave or I would succumb to heart failure, or together we would have to deal in some grievous way with the grinning canine perched in the bow of the canoe, clearly unable to contain his smugness at a situation that found him riding while we pushed, pulled and towed. The wisdom of having an up-to-date life insurance policy was becoming clearer with each laborious step, and it was nearly an hour later, when the water deepened and the vegetation thinned, before we were able to climb aboard again and resume paddling.

Our destination was an island known locally as "Dave's Island," by virtue of the age-old principle of squatter's rights. Having made this island his personal home for two or three weeks every fall for the past several years, Dave had become the uncontested Lord of the Island, thus earning the right to name it. Dave's Island is little more than a couple acres of granite that supports a colourful mix of aspen, birch and spruce trees, and it was here that Dave stashed a canvas wall tent and all the requisite supplies needed to transform the remote isle into a comfortable and hospitable camp for a few weeks every fall. Dave spent as much time on his island as his schedule allowed each fall and was rewarded more often than not with both outstanding waterfowling and a winter's supply of moose meat for the larder.

As Dave had already been out to the island earlier, the tent was up when we arrived; all we had to do before heading out on the water was dump off our food and personal gear. By this time, we were both anxious to check out the diving duck activity, so it was but a 20-minute pit stop and we were back in the canoe, considerably lighter, with Brutus still sporting his grin and well aware what we were off to do. At least this time I got the impression he was smiling with us and not at us. Our destination was a series of islands farther out on the open water of the North Arm, each small enough that you could nearly spit across it. Even as we pushed off, we could see the telltale shallow-winged flights of diving ducks buzzing in and around the outcroppings like flights of spitfires hazing an enemy fleet. Fifteen minutes later, we approached one of the many islands, and Dave simply said, "We're here." I couldn't discern it as being any different than any of the other islands around us, but knew better than to question Dave's experience.

It took us another half-hour to lay out our decoy spread, but what is typically little more than a necessary duck hunting chore is nothing short of inspiring when you watch Dave strategically place his blocks. Accounting for much of the weight in our canoe were four-dozen hand-carved decoys that we positioned in a classic diver set, complete with a well-spaced wing trailing some 200 metres downwind. Carved by renowned London, Ontario, craftsman Ralph Malpage, each individual decoy was both a work of art and a working tool beyond reproach. All were self-righting; each was balanced, shaped and painted to the highest standards. The handsome bluebill and mallard blocks were now sitting exactly where the carver intended them to be, on the water doing what they were designed to do, not adorning someone's mantelpiece as mere conversation pieces. Over many years hunting with Dave, I've come to relish the opportunity to shoot over these blocks as they take me back to a time when duck hunting was infinitely more engaging than the stubble field mallard hunts so prevalent today. The big water and large spreads of hand-crafted decoys represent a waterfowling tradition that is, sadly, fast disappearing.

Once the decoys were out, we parked the canoe and the three of us climbed onto the island, hiding among the natural crevices in the granite carved out by thousands of years of wind and wave action, or crouching behind what little natural shrubbery there was. The relative transparency of our "blinds" mattered little; however, for as long as we remained relatively still, the birds flew with little obvious suspicion. It was evident that none of these birds had been exposed to people, let alone hunters, in many months, if ever. And fly they did. The first wave of bills arced through our spread as if on a strafing run, their cupped wings carving through the air with a singularly familiar sound known only to duck hunters.

As is usually the case, if you hear the birds before you see them, it's too late to shoot, and this flight of 30 birds escaped with nary a feather ruffled nor an eardrum irritated. Dave and I just looked at each other with knowing grins. This was what we'd come for, and the fact that we hadn't even shouldered our shotguns on the first flock in range mattered little to either of us. The thrill of shooting these birds quickly became secondary in importance to soaking up the entire experience.

For those who lust after wilderness waterfowling, let me just say that if you've not lived it firsthand, my feeble attempt to describe it does not do the experience justice. I must confess, however, that Brutus obviously did not share in the romance of the hunt quite like Dave and me. As the first flight roared through our blocks and out to open water, Brutus looked at us with obvious canine disdain. The problem when hunting with an experienced dog is that they can judge distance accurately, and Brutus knew as surely as Dave and I did that the flight of bills had been well within range.

Over the rest of the afternoon, the birds flew steadily on the moderate breezes. More flocks of bills offered us the opportunities to atone for ourselves in Brutus' eyes, though he quickly learned that the fact we were shooting at birds didn't necessarily mean a retrieving opportunity for him when the echoes finally died away. Wedges of ring-necked ducks, the quintessential waterfowl of the boreal wilderness, and Dave's personal favourites, danced through in smaller flocks, their stubby bodies, cheeky attitudes and acrobatic flight capabilities offering little to improve our shell:bird ratio.

Eventually, we grew to learn the necessary leading distances and could more accurately predict from which direction the birds would swing. Over time we splashed our share of birds among the blocks. We at least dropped enough that Brutus no longer appeared ashamed to share a rock with us. On occasion, a flight of mallards or wigeon would swing through for a look on their way to the buffet of the inner marsh, but we invariably passed them up. Although bigger than the birds we were targeting, and certainly fine table fare, their best efforts somehow seemed tame when compared to the blistering pace set by the divers. And for Dave and me, it really wasn't a full stringer of birds that we'd come for.

That first evening, back on Dave's Island, we sat around the campfire, saying little to one another, each recalling the day in the manner that satisfied our needs most. On the campfire grill we seared a couple of plump ringnecks, having first marinated them in a mixture of gin, thyme and coriander. Those who suggest that nothing beats a shore lunch of fresh fish fillets have obviously never savoured the delicate flavour of freshly plucked ring-necked duck cooked over an open flame. Later, we basked in the firelight, the eerie cacophony of migrating sandhill cranes preceding their lithe silhouettes passing across the three-quarter moon. After sipping a nightcap or two while enjoying the free show put on by the northern lights, Dave, Brutus and I snuggled into the comfort of the tent, our beds and our dreams.

The next two days were more of the same. The weather held perfect, with cool mornings and evenings bookending warm middays, and a steady offshore wind that kept the birds moving regularly. We'd put in most of each day on one of the small islands, alternately telling stories, snoozing on the rocks when the sun rose to its highest and shooting when the opportunities presented themselves, though only at those times when we were so inclined to shoot. Daily duck limits in the Northwest Territories are 25 birds per day, per hunter. Had it been our objective, filling a limit would have been no problem, though I suspect we knocked down no more than 15 between us on any day, eating them under the starlight each evening until our bellies could hold no more.

On our paddle towards home on the last day, the section where we were forced to once again slog our way through the dense emergent vegetation somehow seemed less tiring. Brutus seemed less smug. And I no longer felt the urgency to be fully insured. Wilderness duck hunting does that to a man—the aching muscles, full stomach and enriched mind melding into a serenity that has few peers. Perhaps James Swan described it best in his book *In Defense of Hunting* when he said, "Hunters these days ultimately hunt memories as much as meat to put on the table. Memories feed dreams, and hunters must have dreams to keep them motivated. When you lose your dreams, you lose your mind."

I still dream of the Stagg River.

—⚡—

3

GRAYLING: IN THE EYE OF THE BEHOLDER

I have a passion for wilderness, and Arctic grayling thrive only in those places that remain relatively undisturbed by human activity. I'm not clear whether I pursue grayling because they live in cold, clear unspoiled watersheds, or whether I'm attracted first and foremost to those places and have come to appreciate grayling simply because they're there. By most measures the two are inseparable, so I guess it matters little. In any case, I have a decided weakness for these somewhat odd fish. My wife's fondness for fly fishing was born largely on our grayling experiences, and a four- or five-day fly-fishing trip for just the two of us has become an annual affair. For that reason alone, I'll always have a special affection for grayling.

Beauty is a highly subjective notion, yet ironically, one that all of us deem ourselves qualified to opine on authoritatively. Over time I've come to believe that the Arctic grayling personifies all that I consider beautiful in a fish, though I find great difficulty in articulating a defense of this assessment when challenged by those who view it as little more than a whitefish that showed up overdressed to daily roll call. The piscatorial list of traits that typically contribute to a fish ascending to the throne of elegance and desire are, by and large, absent in grayling when evaluated by even the most biased of anglers. They certainly don't boast the symmetric, stylish and sleek lines of those fish that generally come to mind when a more classic definition of beauty is the measuring stick. Rainbow trout, Atlantic salmon and steelhead traditionally sit at the front of the class when assessed with these criteria. The grayling also can't boast the near garish, colourful appearance of Arctic char, brook trout or even sockeye salmon when clad in the ornamental hues of their spawning period. Further, the grayling lacks the brooding, mysterious allure of a brown trout; the playful, "fish-next-door" attractiveness of a smallmouth bass; or the brutish, rogue appeal of a muskie. No, at best the grayling can generously be described as quirkishly pretty. Its mouth is too small, its eyes and scales too large and its sail-like dorsal fin outlandishly ill-suited to its body size.

Despite its obvious physical shortcomings, however, I immediately think of grayling when talk of beautiful fish arises. Upon reflection, maybe it's because I'm an ardent advocate of the Victorian English philosopher of biological and social evolution Herbert Spencer's assertion that, "The

saying that beauty is but skin deep is a skin-deep saying."
Grayling warm my heart, not because of their physical attri-
butes, but rather in spite of them. It is the assemblage of all of
the attributes that define a grayling that bring them so quickly
to mind for me.

My first experience with Arctic grayling came many
years ago when a friend and I paddled a tributary of the burly
Yukon River called the Big Salmon River. The Big Salmon
winds its way from its headwaters at Quiet Lake, adjacent to
the highway between Tagish and Ross River, to its confluence
with the Yukon River near Carmacks. The upper stretch of
the Big Salmon is a carnival ride of rapids, riffles and hairpin
curves, punctuated in the name of adventure by hidden log
jams and sweepers that emerge stealthily from the recesses of
the heavily treed shores.

Within two hours of our departure we'd beached on
the pebbled, inside turn of a right-angled curve in the river.
In part, we stopped to find respite from the exhausting stretch
of river we'd only partway managed. More practically, however, we halted to repair the golf ball–sized hole we'd punched
in the fiberglass hull while trying unsuccessfully to maneuver
our way through a chicane of sunken deadfall. As my partner
set about the repairs with a mixture of superglue and duct
tape, I pulled out my ultralight gear, tied on a Mepps spinner
and tossed the lure into the transition between a riffle and the
corner pool. Immediately I had a fish on, and in no time was
holding aloft a wriggling 14-inch grayling. Three more casts
produced three more fish, and by the time our canoe was
again pronounced fit for duty, we had a fresh-fish supper on
ice in the cooler. For the remainder of that week, cooperative
grayling provided both recreation and sustenance for us, and

it's the fishing fun that comes to mind most readily whenever I think back to that trip.

Grayling are oddly built fish, and while they may not stand up to the most critical aesthetic judgments, they're not without their own array of inherently attractive features. Foremost among these traits is their colouration. Most often described as gray with purplish spots, this pedestrian description does not do justice to the hues of lavender, magenta and lilac that reflect in the right light from their spotted pewter flanks when first pulled from the water. Unfortunately, in keeping with the precedent established by the *Aurora borealis* that shimmers in multi-coloured splendor across the night skies above the waters that grayling call home, the best grayling colours are short-lived. In but a few short seconds after emerging from the water, their complexion loses most of its vibrancy. Blink too long, and you'll miss it.

Even their sail-like dorsal fin has become an endearing feature to me. Much like your favourite uncle with the big nose, you soon fail to see the oversized appendage as a feature unto itself. Eventually, it just becomes one component in a greater whole, and if it were ever to be altered or removed, the remaining composite would be the lesser for it.

One of the grayling memories etched most indelibly in my mind occurred early one morning on a reach of the Stark River at the eastern extreme of Great Slave Lake. We were staying at Frontier Lodge, predominantly fishing for the monster lake trout that ply the lake's frigid depths. But, as an avid fly angler, I didn't want to pass up the chance to tease out a few of the grayling that inhabit the river right below the main lodge. So I slipped down to the river one morning just as dawn broke; a cool August morning and a river full of fish to myself was just too much to resist.

In short order, I'd hooked a pretty decent-sized fish in the 20-inch range, and it was giving me a worthy tussle, taking full advantage of the bubbling rapids above a natural ledge. As I focused on the fish, the wolf was some eight metres into the water before I noticed it. Snow white in colour, the animal had obviously been lured from cover by the struggling fish and had slipped from the cool spruce forest on the far bank to investigate what must have appeared, at first glance, to be an easy meal. The wolf either didn't notice me attached to the other end of the determined grayling, or else it viewed me as a threat worth risking in return for a breakfast of fresh filets.

Upon noticing the wolf's presence and its intentions, I stopped reeling and let the grayling continue to dance at the end of my line. The wolf, no more than 40 metres from where I stood thigh-deep near the opposite bank, was clearly having difficulty with the river. Above the ledge, the turbulent water made it all but impossible for the determined predator to walk out to snag the fish. With every step, he fought to maintain his balance against the rough water. Retreating to shore, he ventured out again, this time into the smooth water below the ledge. But the water's depth forced the wolf to swim, and the current quickly pushed him downriver, again foiling his attempts to close in on his prey. After repeated attempts both above and below the ledge over the course of five minutes, the drenched wolf finally turned away and trotted upstream, offering what appeared to be an indignant shrug of its broad shoulders before disappearing back into the quiet of the forest. It was an experience I would have loved to have shared with someone, but it was somehow made more special for having enjoyed it alone.

Arctic grayling have a reputation for being easy to catch. Although this rep is somewhat undeserved, admittedly there are times when they can be easily fooled, making them an ideal fish for novice anglers. Eager, rather than easy, might be a fairer assessment. It is one such occasion that is probably my favourite recollection of grayling fishing. At the time, my wife Jane had never previously hooked and landed a fish on a fly rod. It was our last day of fishing at the infamous Plummer's Lodge on Great Bear Lake, and instead of another eight hours on the big water in search of lakers, we took up the alternate offer to spend the day on the Sulky River, a quiet grayling stream that spills into the massive lake. We fished less than a mile of the river as it gurgled between two small lakes and literally caught as many grayling as we cared to, tossing #12 elk hair caddis imitations. The river tumbled over a series of ledges, with the pools between the drops as clear as the skies that favoured us that day. Jane landed a couple handfuls of chunky grayling, the best nosing 20 inches and 3 pounds. It would be difficult to imagine a prettier setting for enjoying a first fly-fishing success. The grayling hit our flies with a fervor that suggested they'd seen few artificials in their day, and they fought with a tenacity befitting a creature that lives in a pristine, unspoiled wilderness. I fished one canyon section in the Sulky that still stands as the prettiest piece of water I've yet waded, and to have done it with Jane beside me was sweet icing on an already fulfilling cake.

When all is said and done, I suppose the attraction I have for grayling is as much a reflection of the wild places these fish call home as it is the fish themselves. They are sensitive to disturbance and over-fishing, and where grayling thrive today will tend to be among the most remote and captivating wilderness waters you could hope to discover. I find few things in life as enjoyable as casting to these northern icons under a powder blue sky, with nothing but miles and miles of nothing but miles and miles all around me, and I will continue to seek new opportunities to fish grayling. The lure of the remote waters they call home is an intoxicant with no antidote for those who have fallen under their beguiling spell, and the venerable grayling encapsulates these charms in a simple, dependable and resplendent package. And what could be more beautiful than that?

4

ACADIAN RHYTHM

Brian Hagglund and I became fast friends in high school, which is now more than 40 years in the rear-view mirror. He and his father were my first hunting mentors, and all these many years later we still get together two or three times annually to hunt or fish somewhere. I had never hunted woodcock before this trip and was truly excited by the prospect of marrying a woodcock hunt with fly-casting to Atlantic salmon on the renowned Miramichi River. They go together as effortlessly as peanut butter and jelly, and in my mind, represent the very best of what New Brunswick offers sportsmen.

They say if you walk 50 metres without losing your hat, you're not in good woodcock cover. Given that, my long-time pal Brian Hagglund and I were most definitely in exceptional woodcock cover, in this case, dense young aspens and congested alder tangles thick enough to make a gut-shot brown bear blanch. It's in brushy, young forest habitats such as this that the small, stocky birds spend most of their time, their cryptic plumage rendering them all but invisible.

We were grinding our way through yet another dense thicket when Andrew Anthony, our guide on this New Brunswick upland hunt, once again hollered, "Woodcock!" It was all Brian and I could do to laboriously extract ourselves from our perverse game of outdoor Twister, only to hear the twittering sounds of a timberdoodle headed for safer habitat.

It was our third flush of the morning in the Miramichi River Valley, and I'd yet to lay eyes on my first woodcock. Somehow, I'd imagined that hunting these dapper birds would be a more refined affair in keeping with my impressions of British and New England hunting sensibilities. I was clearly misinformed.

While Andrew was showing remarkable patience and good humour with our awakening to woodcock realities, his six-year old English setter, Snap, would occasionally look our way with what appeared to be canine exasperation and derision. Of course, my guilt and embarrassment at our ineptitude may have clouded my perception.

Fortunately, as the day progressed, so too did our proficiency. The next three birds registered as mere flashes through the trees, but at least I was gaining confidence that woodcock did indeed exist. With the next three flushes, I was able to distinguish a real live bird twisting through, over and around the tangled bushes, though my 20-gauge's barrel was still as clean as it had been when we left nearby Ledges Inn that morning.

Ledges Inn, or simply the Ledges as it's often called, is one of the truly upscale places to stay on the Miramichi River. Seeing the opportunity for a high-end hunting and fishing lodge in the region, sixth-generation locals Everett and Caroline Taylor opened the Ledges in 1996. The four-and-a-half-star venue offers premium accommodations, gourmet dining in a world-class setting and expertly guided hunting and fishing trips. Along with a beautiful view of the river, my room boasted a private bath, fireplace and television, amenities seldom found in a hunting or fishing camp. I suspect there must be clear criteria to meet, but for the life of me I can't imagine what more they could offer to garner that last half star.

By mid-afternoon, when three more woodcock rose from the hawthorn, raspberry and chokecherry understory, I actually shouldered my gun and popped off shots in the general direction of the departing birds. Thankfully, no one was depending on me to bring home supper that evening, but getting a little lead in the air certainly marked some progress. Brian, to his credit, tipped over one of the last flushing woodcock of the day, giving us the first up-close look at our elusive quarry.

We decided to push one last covert for the day when Snap pressured a ruffed grouse from its roost, and I managed to swing and knock it from the sky before it evaporated into the trees. Ever the professional, Andrew was all compliments, offering that grouse are tougher to hit on the wing than wood-cock. Snap, the more honest judge, didn't seem nearly as impressed.

It was the end of our first day, and the score was one woodcock for Brian, one grouse for me, and 13 flushes and nowhere near enough retrieves for Snap. As for Andrew? One gold medal for his patience and perseverance, and for never once letting us see him chuckle.

Our second day on the woodcock trail proved that a couple old dogs can still learn a trick or two. Anthony took Brian and me to some new coverts, former farmsteads that had long been abandoned and grown over and where the fertile, dark soil provided ideal conditions for earthworms, the key food of the resident woodcock. Snap was joined by Tucker, a Brittany spaniel, and the two dogs took turns leading us along.

The cover was as challenging as it had been the day before, but something had changed overnight. It was as though the game had slowed down for us. Not only were we hearing and seeing the birds as the dogs flushed them at Anthony's direction, we were now also able to anticipate how they'd react.

Most often the woodcock would pop straight up until they'd cleared the brush, then fly straight away, albeit twisting and turning all the way. But somehow they weren't nearly as fast as they'd been the day before, allowing us to swing and track them in flight.

Finally, I hit one. Was it my improved shooting or a sign of the apocalypse? I didn't care.

By day's end, Brian and I had collected seven fat woodcock between us, and Anthony presented me with the
"Golden BB," an honorary award for someone who drops
a woodcock with a near-impossible shot. That it was clearly
more luck than skill was something we all agreed to overlook,
though Snap appeared to be eyeing us with renewed respect.

That evening back at Ledges Inn, sipping a sundowner
while listening to the soothing gurgle of the Miramichi, Brian
and I reflected on our two days, content in knowing we hadn't
wasted the amazing opportunities Anthony, Snap and Tucker
had provided.

If there was a time when Brian and I didn't know each
other, it's long been forgotten. Pals since our high school days,
we've seen each other through life's many ups and downs, and
despite having lived two provinces apart for the last 30 years,
it's as though no time has passed whenever we get together. We
try to hunt or fish together at least a couple times every year, so
when the invitation came to experience the fishing and hunting out of Ledges Inn in the Miramichi River Valley, it was only
natural that he'd join me.

In the morning we'd be switching gears completely,
putting down our shotguns and picking up fly rods to tackle
the undisputed king of Canadian sportfish: the Atlantic
salmon.

There's nothing like the dawn. The half-hour before
the curtain is lifted on a new day is an intense experience,
overflowing with anticipation. Greeting us at first light was
Serge Collin, a travel media representative with the Province

of New Brunswick. He'd joined us for two days of fishing with Ledges guide Rodney Colford, who welcomed the three of us with a hearty hello.

In his late 40s, Rodney grew up on the Miramichi and its 37 tributaries. He began guiding salmon anglers at age 18, mentored in the industry by his father, Gary, a lifelong guide who had also been introduced to guiding by *his* father. Rodney was the quintessential guide: equal parts teacher, events director and friend to his sports. He had the relaxed demeanor of someone who knows his craft and is eager to share what he knows.

That first day, we fished the Cains River, a well-known Miramichi tributary ideal for inexperienced salmon anglers. It's big enough to hold good numbers of salmon, yet small enough that you can wade out and cover all the good pools.

We hadn't been fishing long when Serge locked onto a fish. The day's first catch is always an upbeat event, confirming that fish are present and willing to strike. So with more encouragement than was needed, the three of us cheered on Serge until Rodney slid the big landing net under a stunning 14-pound male, its jutting kype confirming it was a fresh fish heading upstream to spawn.

Throughout the rest of the day, we worked promising-looking pools and runs, changing spots and flies as the mood struck us or as Rodney suggested. We experimented with a range of tried-and-true salmon flies; Green Machines, Ally's Shrimps, Black Bear Green Butts, Marabou Leeches and more were all given the chance to entice a fish.

Around mid-afternoon, I had a sharp tug on a Green Machine. It was definitely a fish striking, but I came up empty only a few seconds into the fight. Eventually, dusk arrived, and it was time to head back to the lodge.

Fly-fishing Atlantic salmon is a big boy's game. The first time out, you get your butt kicked, and all you can do is dust yourself off and try again. And again. Eventually, if you're persistent and patient enough, you'll hook a fish. And inevitably, you'll fall in love with salmon fishing. That had happened to me years earlier on Ungava's George River, and it was plain to see that Brian, despite not hooking a fish, was also falling under the spell of the legendary "leaper."

Before dinner back at Ledges, we took a quick drive into nearby Doaktown to visit W.W. Doak, the famed fly-fishing shop that's been serving anglers in the region since 1946. There's something about local tackle shops that make you just want to hang out. Perhaps it's the history, imagining all the famous anglers who have stepped across its threshold. Maybe it's just the buzz, the constant chatter among staff and patrons, the tales of fish caught and fish lost. Or perhaps it's simply the appeal of all the spanking new tackle, wall-to-wall rods, reels, flies, waders and more.

In any case, Doak's has great character, and we both grabbed a few flies before leaving. Among the flies I selected was a non-traditional pattern called the Same Thing Murray, which came with an interesting history. A few years earlier, so the story goes, a visiting salmon angler, frustrated with his lack of success, tied an off-the-cuff pattern one evening. As luck would have it, he caught a fish with it the very next morning.

"What did you catch him on," hollered his partner, fishing across the river.

"That pattern I tied last night," replied the lucky angler. He would go on to catch two more fish, and when his friend asked for the third time what he was using, he replied, "The same thing, Murray!" The name stuck, and now the fly is being tied commercially.

As it turned out, it was a good thing I bought one.

We spent our last day in New Brunswick on the Miramichi River itself, and we were stoked to get started. Since the 1800s, the Miramichi has rightfully staked its claim as North America's finest salmon river. Annual runs can approach 100,000 fish, the largest on the continent, and those in the know say that it's responsible for 50 percent of all rod-caught Atlantic salmon each year.

Shortly after first light, Rodney eased our canoe—traditional river transport on the Miramichi—upstream to Flo's Pool, one of the more famous salmon reaches that Ledges' guides visit. Serge, Brian and I were spaced through-out the pool and began the repetitive down-and-across casting that is the standard presentation.

Salmon heading upstream to spawn feed little, but they'll occasionally strike out of aggression. So, the only thing an angler can do is keep on casting. An hour in, Serge hooked up and eventually brought an 11-pound hen to bay. Less than an hour later, he was into another fish, this time a grilse.

After lunch, our spirits buoyed by Serge's success, we moved farther upstream to a long pool known as The Rocks. Once again, we divided up the run then cast our flies into every likely looking piece of water. By 3:30 PM, with the fish in an uncooperative mood, it was beginning to look like Brian and I would be shut out, not an uncommon experience with Atlantic salmon but disappointing, nonetheless.

As a last resort, I decided to tie on the Same Thing Murray that I'd picked up at Doak's. It was only on my second cast when, salmon being salmon, I had a strike when I expected it least, at the tail end of a drift and well beyond what I figured was the fish-holding water. At the take, I struck back firmly and knew immediately the fight was on.

With Rodney coaching me along, Brian taking pictures and Serge cheering, I carefully played the fish. Four times it leapt clear of the water, and each time I bowed to the fish, remembering hard-won lessons from previous salmon battles. When it wanted to run, I let it, twice taking me well into my backing as my reel sang to the rhythm of the fish's pulses.

Both times it grudgingly gave me back my line, and after a 15-minute tussle, I backed the fish carefully into the net Rodney slid under its weary form. As he knelt to remove the fly, I let out a whoop that I'm sure reverberated five kilometres in every direction. There's just something about landing a wild Atlantic salmon that calls for celebration, even one as rudimentary as an undignified "Yahoo!"

The fish was magnificent, a mature hen that Rodney estimated at 15 pounds. After the requisite photo op, I tailed the fish into the current as she regained her strength, and in just a couple of minutes she flicked her tail once and slid back into the darkness of the river.

We fished another hour that afternoon, though I must admit that, in the afterglow of my first Miramichi salmon, I wasn't quite as sharp as I'd been earlier. Serge, on the other hand, continued to enjoy what he later described as the single best day's fishing he has ever enjoyed, hooking and releasing another salmon and a second grilse.

Fittingly that evening, the Ledges' renowned chef, Luc Schofield, prepared one of his award-winning traditional New Brunswick meals—duck confit and fiddleheads. It was the perfect dessert to our four-day main course of woodcock and Atlantic salmon, and I can't wait for another taste of it all.

—◊—

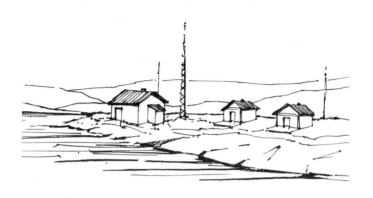

5

DREAMS ABOVE THE ARCTIC CIRCLE

In one of his last acts as editor of *Outdoor Canada* magazine, James Little asked me if I would be willing to take on an assignment to write about Plummer's Lodge on Great Bear Lake. Not that it was an onerous task, in fact, it was more of a going-away present from him to me. Better yet, I was welcome to take along my then-girlfriend, Jane. I've long-believed that the allure of the Arctic and the experience we shared on this trip contributed significantly to her eventually becoming my wife. For that I'll always be grateful to James.

Great Bear Lake. Tree River. Horton River. Katseydie River. Their names are spoken in hushed tones throughout the angling world, and not just because they are renowned fishing waters. In their frigid depths, as the record books clearly show, lurk the largest fish of their kind in the world: Lake trout capable of swallowing the largest pike whole; Arctic char whose sheer will to survive has left many an angler staring glumly at the shattered remains of their tackle; and Arctic grayling, the eager ones, the stout dancers with iridescent bodies of purple and silver. I've known about these places all my fishing life, as have most ardent anglers, and many times I've dreamed of standing on their barren, windswept shores and cobbled bottoms, rod in hand.

It's little wonder I could barely contain my excitement as our plane crossed the Arctic Circle and touched down on the gravel airstrip along the eastern shore of Great Bear Lake's Dease Arm. I had trophy fish in mind and couldn't wait to get on the water. First up was Great Bear and its legendary lakers then a fly-out to Tree River for Arctic char; time constraints meant the Horton and the Katseydie might have to wait for another visit.

After settling into our room at Plummer's Great Bear Lake Lodge—mere metres from the swells lapping along the rocky shore—Jane and I ate a quick lunch then got our tackle pulled together, only to discover our assigned guide was ill and unable to take us out. Anxious as we were to start our week of fishing, we had to wait for the other guides to return from their day trips. At least the delay allowed us time to familiarize ourselves with the lodge and its facilities. Plus, the free afternoon gave me a chance to meet celebrated lodge owner, Chummy Plummer.

When Chummy shakes your hand, he smiles like a man who knows a lot more than he's letting on. Chummy has been guiding in the north since he was 13, and along with his father, Warren, he's kept the guiding business going on Great Bear Lake, always able to stay one step ahead of the challenges that have claimed other lodges in the Northwest Territories. Despite the difficulties associated with running northern lodges (Plummer's owns three operations on Great Bear and one each on Great Slave Lake and Tree River), Chummy remains almost inexplicably serene. He is also remarkably down to earth.

Although his guest list over the years has included the who's who of fishing enthusiasts, Chummy is not one to put on airs. When I asked him to list some of his more famous clients over the years, he was genuinely at a loss for names. "Oh, I don't know. George Bush, I guess. Some other politicians. Bob Hope. Lots of movie stars, but I can't remember their names," he replied. "Up here, they all get treated the same." For Chummy, there's only one priority when it comes to his guests: "I like making others happy."

At around 6:00 PM, the camp's other guests and their guides began to return to the lodge for dinner before quickly heading out again. Not being able to swap stories with them only added to our growing anxiety, so it was with great relief that camp manager Cameron Baty found us a guide for the evening stint. Mike was a university student and avid angler from Sault Ste. Marie, Ontario, who'd found the summer gig of his dreams. As it turned out, he was representative of half the 25 or more full-time guides in camp. The other half were retired or semi-retired, now enjoying some wilderness after a lifetime in the working world down south.

We hit Great Bear's waters knowing that a trophy laker could strike at any time, but by 1:00 AM we accepted the fact that you can get shut out even on the best waters of the planet some days. The 45-minute-long sunset—a glorious apricot sphere slinking its way down through an indigo sky—was reward enough for us.

The next two full days presented more of the same. Our originally assigned guide, Adam, had recovered from his ailment and worked us hard from first light to last, exploring every nook and cranny, sunken island, drop-off, sand flat and boulder field he knew. Surprisingly, despite the fact that at least 10 other boats floated on the water each day, we never saw another fishing party, a testament to the enormity of this great lake.

Jane and I caught plenty of fish both days, though none you'd describe as trophies by Great Bear's standards, where 30- and 40-pound fish hardly lift eyebrows. We knew those fish were there, though, as each night we heard the stories and watched as the names of the guests who had landed trophies went up on the board in the lounge. Since they were doing the same thing we were, trolling Huskie Devles and T-60 Flatfish, we just figured the fishing gods simply weren't with us.

Nonetheless, we were having fun. Our daily shore lunches were superb; the natural beauty of the rugged backdrop was stunning; and caribou, wolves, bald eagles and loons offered regular sightings. The only complaints were those lodged by our backs after long days pounding across the unceasing swells, but a good night's sleep always had us eager to get back at it the following morning. Besides, Great Bear generally produces only one 50-pound lake trout for every 1500 trolling hours, so tough slogging is to be expected. Unless, of course, a visiting angler gets lucky like the Vegas gambler who hits the jackpot with the drop of his first nickel. It happens with enough regularity that you can't help but dream you're next.

On the fourth day, Cameron asked us if we'd like to go on an overnight excursion to the Tree River Camp in the neighbouring territory of Nunavut. The Tree is a relatively short river running north to the Arctic Ocean just east of the 1300-person hamlet of Kugluktuk, formerly known as Coppermine. Before we even left home I had been looking forward to fishing the Tree—home to the world-record 32.5-pound Arctic char—so we readily agreed to the 90-minute flight in a 1943-vintage DC-3.

Although I've been fortunate enough to spend many months in Canada's Barren Lands, this was Jane's first visit. And like all neophytes, her first impression was one of awe. And surprise. Expecting to see a barren landscape, as the area's name implies, visitors instead find surging torrents of jade-coloured water and veins of smooth granite slicing neatly through lush, rolling hills of green.

Upon landing on the graveled strip, our Inuk guide met us at the river's edge, grinning broadly from under an oversized cowboy hat. "Hi, I'm John Wayne," he said, and somehow I knew our fortunes were about to improve. After a quick boat ride upriver to camp for an inspiring char lunch, we geared up and headed out.

The prime fishing on the Tree lies within a three-kilometre stretch upstream of camp where the river is punctuated by three sets of falls, the largest of which is roughly six metres high. As we walked along the well-worn path, John pointed out the various pools and islands, each with its own name and morsel of colourful history. One of the places where we tried our luck was the Presidential Pool, so named because former U.S. President George Bush landed a char there in 1995.

A pocket of slow water some 30 metres wide by 45 metres long, the Presidential Pool is a prime resting spot for char making their tiring upstream spawning run through the furious waters of the main channel. I could see the occasional fin break the rippled surface as I tied on a heavy spoon, and for the next 15 minutes, I fan-casted the pool without so much as the slightest resistance on my line.

Try across the pool by that big rock," John offered. I responded by making a long cast in the direction he was pointing.

The scarlet char knew it was hooked before I did, announcing itself by launching skyward in a frothy spray. I had yet to collect my wits when the fish made its second aerial appearance, and before I could stammer out a single word, it spit the hook. I just stood there in disbelief; I'd hooked up with a 15-pound-or-better char on the Tree River and lost it. But I'm nothing if not persistent, so I lobbed out my spoon again, this time with the concentration and commitment that only comes with the confidence of knowing fish are present.

Over the next two hours, I had the time of my fishing life. I hooked into five more fin-powered rockets, but despite my best efforts, only managed to beach two. These were unlike any fish I'd ever tangled with before. They were wild creatures whose very souls compelled them to remain free at any cost. Once hooked, they immediately took to the air in a valiant effort to escape, displaying a repertoire of twists and spins that would shame an Olympic diver. And if aerial combat failed them, their backup plan was to make a return tear to the turbulent waters of the river's main stem.

Even with 20-pound test, it was clear we were outgunned, a fact made evident after I'd broken two lines and shattered one graphite rod. Despite the fact that we were clearly coming out second best, the three of us sported grins that couldn't have been stretched any wider with a tractor. And by the time we continued up the path beyond the pool, I was completely worn out from the combination of non-stop action, laughing like a fool and cursing like a sailor deprived of shore leave. I later hooked two more char on jigs, landing one, while Jane fought another crimson beauty to a standstill, only to lose it at her feet.

Before heading back to Great Bear at noon the next day, we boated down to where the Tree meets the Arctic Ocean. Along the way we were treated to the inspiring sight of a barren-ground grizzly swimming effortlessly across the one-and-a-half-kilometre-wide river mouth. Then, to prove God knows what, Jane and I jumped hand-in-hand into the frigid waters of the Arctic Ocean, only to emerge shivering uncontrollably. Following our act of bone-chilling bravado, it became clear why fly-outs to Tree River typically last just 24 hours—any more unrestrained fun could kill a person.

During our flight back to Great Bear, it became clear that our luck had changed; we'd done considerably better than any of the other guests on our excursion. We could only hope that luck would follow us back to Great Bear. But it was not to be. In fact, it got worse, even as the list of names on the 20-pound-plus honour roll grew steadily longer.

For starters, a heavy fog forced us to turn back from an attempted fly-out to Branson's, an old lodge on Great Bear that Plummer's uses as an outpost camp. It had reportedly been surrendering some big lakers, but now we'd have to fish within boating distance of the main lodge. So, off we went again with our Great Bear guide, Adam. After a couple of hours trolling and only two small trout to show for our efforts, I suggested we take a break and explore a small, rocky island. Good idea, poor execution.

While the three of us were playing Indiana Jones, our trusty boat decided to head off on an adventure of its own. It was only when I heard Jane hollering from one end of the 100-metre-long islet that I realized what was happening. I ran across the rocks just in time to see Adam, sopping wet, swimming back to shore after failing to retrieve our wayward boat. By then it was 60 metres out and drifting away with the wind; in those hypothermia-inducing waters, it may as well have been a kilometre away.

Luckily, another guide happened along an hour or so later and graciously rescued us. Otherwise, we might have spent the rest of the day, if not the entire frigid night, as castaways. Our good fortune held out somewhat for the balance of the afternoon; however, and we landed nearly 20 fish. While none pushed the Toledos to the weight required to get us on the board at the lodge, several were close enough that we were more than satisfied.

Our last day left us with a choice. The first option was to try, once more, to hook into one of the gargantuan lakers that have made Great Bear famous. Option two was to fly out to the tiny Sulky River to fish for Arctic grayling. It was a tough decision. During the week we'd been in camp, after all, Great Bear had served up 97 lake trout that surpassed the 20-pound threshold. Of those, one was an unofficial world record, weighing in at a whopping 78 pounds. Then there were two fish that topped 60 pounds, as well as a 57-pounder and two more listed at more than 40 pounds.

While we were due for some luck with the lake trout, we decided instead to try our hand at the grayling, so off we flew in the camp's Cessna on floats. One of the prettiest streams I've ever seen, the Sulky features broad expanses of flat water, tumultuous riffles and a gorgeous waterfall, all jammed into less than three kilometres of river. And the weather couldn't have been any better.

It was Jane's first attempt at fly-fishing, and her natural athletic ability soon had her casting well enough to fool one grayling after another. I lost count of the number of chunky grayling that slurped our caddisfly imitations off the surface without so much as a second thought, the best of them nearing 20 inches and an estimated three pounds. After several days of big tackle, big water and tough fish, the delicate presentation of a dry fly and the sprightly resistance of a dancing grayling offered a welcomed respite, and a fantastic way for the two of us to spend our last day together in the Arctic. It couldn't have been more enjoyable. And I'm pretty sure that's the way Chummy Plummer wanted us to feel.

—◊◊◊—

6

BULLS AND BEARS ON THE BARRENS

If Canadians had to select two large mammals to represent what our country is all about, grizzly bears and caribou might well be them. We're a nation that prides itself on retaining much of our natural beauty and healthy populations of what are commonly referred to as "charismatic megafauna." I went on this excursion eagerly anticipating hunting a vast population of migrating caribou. I certainly wasn't expecting that I would see a grizzly bear, much less have to engage with one. But that's one of the rewards of exploring Canada's wilderness; you never know what might be lurking around the corner. While my vision of seeing thousands upon thousands of caribou gliding effortlessly across the landscape was realized, sadly that is no longer the case. Caribou herds across Canada and beyond are in decline, and the scientific community isn't clear why or what they can do to arrest the situation.

Sitting in the bow of the 14-foot aluminum boat, I buried my face in the collar of my parka. Waves of nausea swept through me, steadily increasing in strength and regularity as we bounced over Jolly Lake's September swells. I lifted my face only occasionally and then simply to blow out my clogged sinuses, cough or suck in some fresh Arctic air in an attempt to quell the nausea. No question about it, I was sick, and this was just day one of a 12-day hunt for Central Canada Barren Ground Caribou. I floundered in my despair as memories of a recent caribou hunt wormed their way through my phlegm-clogged mind. On that trip, to Québec's Ungava Peninsula, I stared through the window of my outfitter's Kuujjuaq home for five days, crestfallen, as sleet, snow and rain pounded on the fragile window pane. Eventually, I flew home, dejected, never having seen the caribou camp we were to have flown in to. I wrote that experience off as bad luck. Weather is a hunter's cruel mistress, and you must always be prepared to accept the cards her fickle fingers deal. But now, as I huddled against another cold, northern wind, I began to wonder if I somehow wasn't destined for another disappointing journey for the most iconic of all Canada's antlered game.

I first met Don Cadieux at the local sportsman's show, where he had taken a booth to promote his guiding operation. We talked at some length about his camp and the caribou that migrated through the area each fall, and left promising to stay in touch. I wasn't totally surprised then when he called four months later. Was I still interested in coming up? A break in his schedule had left an opening with no other hunters in camp, but I had to be willing to stay for 12 days instead of the typical three or four. In my mind that just made the possibility all that much more attractive, and I readily agreed. A friend, Leo Gariepy, had always wanted to hunt barren-ground caribou and he, too, jumped at the opportunity when I called.

Our transportation into Don's camp, a Single Otter on floats, lifted powerfully off the water at Yellowknife harbour before swinging northeast for the 250-kilometre flight to Jolly Lake. Besides Leo, myself, and our pilot, onboard was an odd assortment of cargo, including food, camping gear, lumber and oil heaters—typical fare for a remote camp whose supplies must all be brought in by air. Thousands of lakes dotted the wild landscape below, and the spruce forests gradually gave way to tundra, where rock, lichens, mosses and shrubs dominated. Stunted trees, unable to cope with the harsh northern climate, found refuge only in select valleys, where protection from the winds and an adequate moisture regime allowed them to eke out a meagre existence.

The wind was up as we hit the lake and drifted to the small dock below camp, where the smiling faces of four successful hunters greeted us as we settled to a stop. As is accepted protocol, we all pitched in to unload then reload the aircraft with the impressive racks of several good caribou, the crowning glory to the cargo. As the plane lifted off the lake, we turned and headed up the short slope to the buildings where, after unpacking our gear, we hoisted a mug of camp coffee and got to know our hosts.

Don had just one guide in at the time, Peppy Beaulieu, a Chippewa from Fort Resolution. Peppy would quickly prove just how skilled he was, with his knowledge of the local wildlife, his hunting prowess, his deft ability around the kitchen and his easy-going, infectious way with clients. It was readily apparent that this would be a relaxing, enjoyable hunting camp atmosphere.

Day two started in a rush, with the excited shouts of my hosts stirring me from my slumber. I scrambled out of the tent and followed their pointing arms to a lone wolf, ambling slowly across the tundra some 400 metres away. I'd brought along a wolf tag, so quickly rooted through my bags to locate shells, unpacked my rifle and settled in to take the shot. By this time the wolf was probably 450 metres distant, but I decided to give him one try as he appeared to be a large, well-furred male. At the crack of the gun, the wolf jumped then trotted ahead 10 metres or so before stopping again.

"You were just below him. Shoot again!" urged Peppy. But I'd already decided to let him go; he was far enough away that the shot was no certainty, and I didn't want to risk wounding and losing him. Instead, I gathered up my rifle, changed out of my pajamas and headed for the main building where breakfast awaited.

I'm probably using the term "building" a little loosely. Camp consisted of one large tent-frame structure, with wooden floors and walls covered by a tarp roof, that served as kitchen/lounging room/office; a smaller tent-frame building where Leo and I slept; and a steel granary, transported up from the wheat belt of the prairies, where Don and Peppy slept. Despite its spartan appearance, camp was comfortable, with oil heaters in every building ensuring warmth against the tundra's unpredictable weather.

It was at breakfast that I first discovered I wasn't feeling quite up to par, and I settled into the boat's bow quite content to allow Leo first crack at any caribou we might find. Hunting at Jolly Lake is similar to caribou hunting across much of the Arctic. Most of the time is spent cruising the shoreline, glassing the surrounding barrens for signs of migrating caribou and occasionally beaching to climb natural high points to assist in the spotting effort. Whenever we located caribou we'd glass them carefully, looking for potential trophy-class bulls. In this respect we relied on Peppy's guidance for the first few days but soon learned what antler characteristics to look for when evaluating bulls. To the uninitiated, all caribou bulls look big, and they are when judged by the standards set by smaller-racked animals such as the deer of the south. But looks can be deceiving, and the subtle nuances of spread, top points, bez, shovels and back points must be learned to accurately differentiate average-sized from trophy bulls.

The caribou we were hunting were part of the Bathurst herd, which at the time numbered some 350,000 animals. These animals summer adjacent to Bathurst Inlet on the Arctic Ocean and migrate southwest to the treeline for the winter. In fact, most Central Canada Barren Ground Caribou hunted are part of the migrating Bathurst herd, including those in the renowned Courageous Lake and Mackay Lake areas.

Somehow I managed to survive that first day of hunting without losing my lunch, likely a poor choice of words considering I couldn't bring myself to actually eat, opting instead to snooze on a rock shelf while Leo and Peppy scoured the horizon for signs of moving caribou while munching on their sandwiches.

Fortunately, by the third day I was feeling better. We'd taken no caribou at that point, despite having looked over several hundred in our search for a wall hanger. I was in no hurry, but Leo was getting a little antsy; it takes a strong constitution to hold off with so many respectable trophies within easy range. Mid-afternoon on day three we spotted four bulls that warranted further inspection, so we beached the boat and stalked to within 80 metres of where they huddled. We looked them over for a full 20 minutes; it was easy to tell which was the best of the lot but difficult to make the decision about shooting or not. Leo eventually decided to take him, and the bull fell at the report of his 7mm Rem. Mag. As always, it was a combination of joy and relief to see some success in camp.

That evening I took my shotgun out for a three-kilometre walk north of camp and managed to collect a brace of ptarmigan and an arctic hare. The trio would provide us a superb meal the following day under Peppy's culinary guidance. My walkabout was a reflection of one of the most enjoyable aspects of Don's camp; he never got too excited about scheduling the day's activities. We hunted for as long as we liked at the hours we preferred. Peppy was always keen to go whenever we were.

Early the next evening, things in camp began to get real interesting. I was reading in bed when I heard Max, Don's young husky, woof a loud warning. I leapt out of the tent, meeting Peppy and Don as they emerged from the kitchen, just in time to see a large boar grizzly gallop over a rise and out of sight a couple hundred metres from camp. It was thrilling to encounter such a large bear, certainly the top of the food chain in this harsh ecosystem. Despite having encountered several dozen grizzly bears over the years, each sighting is as inspiring as the first, especially in such non-traditional grizzly habitat.

The following day was a near mirror image—a long day's hunt looking over numerous caribou, a decision to continue to hold off and an unwelcome evening visitor. The wind was howling that night, muffling all other noise, but Max's warning stirred Leo nonetheless. He, in turn, woke me with a start. I could immediately make out Max's muted barks, grabbed my shotgun and a flashlight, and stumbled out into the dark. There, not 30 metres away, and parked beneath the metal racking heavily laden with the meat from Leo's caribou, sat another grizzly bear. This one appeared smaller than the previous evening's but was no more welcome when it came to dining on our fine steaks. I yelled at the bear, who responded by bouncing forward a few steps before turning back and taking up station beneath the meat once again. I hollered at the complacent bruin again and again, all to no avail. Not wanting to waste any more sleep time, or further risk our meat, I slipped a "cracker" shell into my over/under, aimed a few feet over the bear's back and touched off the trigger.

The projectile emerged from the barrel with a whoosh, and I could follow its glowing light as it traversed the black air between where I stood and the grizzly. It exploded with a crack almost directly above the bear who, obviously frightened, departed at full throttle, disappearing into the dark and wind of the Arctic night. The noise from the howling north wind was so loud that Don and Peppy never stirred from their slumber despite me discharging a shotgun a mere 20 metres from where they slept.

In the morning, Leo and I related our story to a concerned Don. He cautioned us to be vigilant at night and to be sure not to injure or kill any visiting grizzly except as an absolute last, life-saving, resort. We were later to learn that grizzly bears are a problem for many of the northern caribou camps, and that some operators are not as patient and sensitive to these great bears as Don is. Shooting them is the easy, unethical and often illegal way out of a bear problem.

As we might have guessed, however, we'd barely finished supper that evening after another long day of hunting when what was becoming an all-too-familiar noise startled us. We emerged from the kitchen just in time to see the meat rack collapse on top of a surprised bear. At first, it looked as if the bear was imprisoned in the tangle of metal, but he quickly rose and simply walked through the heavy aluminum bars as though they were spider webs. We repacked the meat and cape from Leo's caribou to more secure quarters, short a few steaks I might add, and settled in for the night. It proved to be a fitful sleep; however, as old *Ursus arctos* paid us two more unwelcome visits that night.

The next few days were successful from several standpoints; Leo shot a second caribou, I took my first and the local bears allowed us consecutive nights of undisturbed sleep. We fished for a few hours, taking a good number of Arctic grayling on both fly and spinning gear, along with several lake trout, including a trophy-class specimen that Leo hooked right from the dock. Both of us also managed to down a few ptarmigan with our smoothbores; this was fast becoming a real "cast-and-blast" adventure. On the downside, Leo picked up the bug I'd had earlier in the week and was feeling pretty rough. But with his two caribou tags filled, he could afford to spend a couple easy days close to camp.

Our hunt was to end on a Sunday afternoon; on Friday morning I still had a tag to fill. I put too many hard miles on my boots that day to count, choosing to hunt on foot instead of from the water. The heavy wind and constant rain actually made for good, albeit uncomfortable, hunting conditions. Around our typical dinner hour, Peppy and I made a long stalk on seven huge bulls bedded together in a small depression. All would have easily made Boone and Crockett's record books; two of them would have placed very high. Poor decision-making got the best of me, and in an effort to close the gap "just a little bit more," I inadvertently spooked one of the bulls. They were all up and gone before I had time to think or blink, much less get off a reasonable shot with the black-powder rifle I was toting. We wandered back to camp well after dark at the conclusion of a long day afield, completely satisfied despite not having filled a tag.

In the middle of the night, I once again awoke to Max's barking, and expecting we'd had a return visit from one of the by-now-familiar bears, strode out into the screaming wind and blowing rain armed with my shotgun and flashlight. Despite my efforts, I saw nothing and returned quickly to the comfort of my bed and some much-needed sleep. The next morning, however, tracks in the sand told the whole story. A sow and two cubs had indeed visited under the cover of darkness, dining royally on the meat from two caribou that had once hung on what was now an irreparable meat rack. Two full caribou carcasses gone, just like that.

That bear encounter added pressure to my Saturday hunt. Despite having three beautiful racks to show for our efforts, we now had the meat from only one animal stored safely away, and both Leo and I were counting heavily on filling our freezers with succulent caribou meat. But, as long and hard a day as Peppy and I put in that Saturday, we didn't see a 'bou I really wanted to take. The migration was in full swing through the area at this point, gracing us with the spectacle of wave after wave of caribou striding slowly but steadily over the uneven tundra in their ground-eating manner along the lakeshore. Yet, despite my desire to collect some meat for home, I simply wasn't interested in taking an animal below the trophy standards I'd set. At least not yet. The plane to take us out wasn't due until noon the next day, leaving me the morning to give it one last stab.

I awoke with a start at about 3:00 AM to the most frantic barking I'd heard yet from Max. Leo and I went out into the teeth of what was fast becoming a full-on fall blizzard. There, no more than six metres away, was a grizzly with his head buried in our camp garbage bucket. To my amazement, Max was tethered a metre away, going absolutely out of his mind, barking, yelping and doing backflips in his attempt to run off the bear. But the young grizzly seemed not to care in the least, totally ignoring the territorial husky he could have dispatched with a single swat of his paw without having to move from where he stood. Don intentionally kept the garbage next to Max's tether for that very reason, so he wouldn't have to worry about wild animals disturbing it before it could be flown out for proper disposal. Was he going to be in for a surprise!

I hollered at the bear, who ignored me entirely, then hit him with a well-aimed stone to the rump; he barely looked up to acknowledge my presence. Leo fired a shot from his rifle into the air; still no reaction. At this point I decided to go for reinforcements, and putting my head into the gale force wind, pushed my way to Don and Peppy's granary, explaining the situation to them. The bear was still out there, continuing to ignore me, so I figured I'd treat him with the same indifference and headed back to bed. In any case, it was miserable outside, and the comfort of my warm sleeping bag was inviting. Knowing I'd hear the rest of the story at breakfast, I was sound asleep in no time.

At breakfast I learned that Don and Peppy had spent a couple hours on guard patrol, eventually chasing the bear out of camp for good. More importantly, however, this was the last day of my hunt, the last few hours in fact, and I still wanted to collect another good caribou or at least give it the old college try. But the weather was the worst it had been all week, blowing hard, alternatively raining and snowing. Peppy looked at me and I at him. Silently, we both agreed that we'd much rather be on the tundra hunting than sitting in camp, particularly with the chore of packing up to be completed by whoever was in camp. So we bundled up in our warmest clothing and headed down the lake.

We returned to camp just three hours later with the biggest caribou of the week packed solidly into the bow of the boat. My perseverance had paid off, and Peppy's skills as a guide had once again proven themselves. His ability to render a freshly killed animal to cape, antlers and manageable chunks of boneless meat was truly amazing to witness. To top it off, we made it back to camp a full hour before the Otter was due to take us back to Yellowknife—not even close by hunting standards.

As it turned out, the inclement weather delayed the plane for five hours, but the down time allowed me to reflect on our days in camp. It had been a rewarding adventure in a picture-perfect landscape. The bears and other wildlife were just added seasoning to a stew of good fun, great company and exceptional hunting. I was reminded that there aren't many places left where a hunter can still experience a wild, rugged, hostile and unspoiled environment in such comfort, however primitive and simple. Jolly Lake indeed.

—〰—

7

MUSKWA COUNTRY ELK

I've known Perry McCormick since our college days in Lethbridge, Alberta. We've hunted together almost every year since, and I think of him not only as a good friend but also as a mentor. In particular, it was Perry who first introduced me to fly-fishing, a pastime that's provided me with countless hours of enjoyment since he first showed me how to handle the "high line." Together we were invited to BC's Muskwa River country to hunt elk and to experience first hand the growing conflict between outfitters and packers. While we did gain an understanding of that dispute, more importantly, we came away from this trip with a whole new appreciation for horses, the beauty of the high country and how large game populations can thrive when afforded the opportunity to live in virtually untouched wilderness.

The Cessna 172 banked sharply as it crested the plateau and dropped into the mountain valley. Below us lay northeastern BC's Muskwa River valley, a Mecca of sorts to those who are afflicted with elk fever. The reasons were obvious; vast tracts of cool, dark spruce forests gave way in their upper reaches to sparse stands of pine and broad expanses of virginal grasslands. Cold, clear creeks knifed winding paths from their birthplaces high in the peaks through the timber, spilling in frothy explosions into the serpentine river. You could almost smell the elk, even from our lofty vantage some 600 metres above the valley floor. I turned to my hunting partner, Perry, and smiled; there could be no doubt that we were headed directly into the heart of prime elk habitat.

"So, where do we land?" I innocently inquired of the pilot.

Never taking his eyes from the windscreen, he replied somewhat tersely, "See that sand bar by the big bend in the creek? That's where we'll put her down."

It didn't look big enough to pitch a tent to me, but I figured he must know what he's doing and sat quietly, allowing myself a quick sideways glance at Perry. The look on his face perfectly mirrored the feeling in my guts.

Without losing his intense focus, the pilot broke the silence. "Do you see that big burned out area up above the south creek bank? That's where a plane went down two years ago trying to land on this same bar. It was too bad. I knew the guy, and he was a good backcountry pilot."

Our pilot obviously had never taken a public relations course. Either that or he just wanted to see how pale he could get his passengers before getting them to safe ground.

I quickly checked my seat belt and put on my bravest face, smiling meekly at Perry. Looking forward, I noticed something taped to the dashboard of the Cessna. Upon closer inspection, it revealed itself to be a passage from the Bible. I didn't know if that was a good or bad thing to see under the circumstances, as I'm not particularly religious, but I figured it never hurts to have God as your co-pilot.

The plane banked and set up for final approach. Bucking against the winds that always seem to buffet small aircraft at critical times, the pilot guided her firmly, yet smoothly, through the creek canyon, putting her down on the leading edge of the sand bar surprisingly lightly given the condition of the runway (or lack thereof). As we came to a complete stop, I grinned weakly at Perry through sweat-soaked lips then stepped confidently out the door onto good old *terra firma*.

We had been invited to spend 12 days on a horse pack trip for elk in the upper reaches of Gathto Creek, a tributary to the infamous Muskwa. Our host, Robert, was a packer, different from an outfitter in that he was only allowed to take BC resident hunters out. On top of that, by law, packers weren't allowed to "guide" hunters in the truest sense of the word; they were permitted only to transport people and gear into and out of the back country. Clients must hunt of their own accord once they are in camp. As we were soon to discover, that is not a particularly challenging endeavour once you're in this game-rich wilderness.

We spent the first couple days in base camp, fishing grayling and bull trout in the creek and familiarizing ourselves with the horses and tack. I'd had virtually no previous experience with horses, Perry little more. Commencing on this adventure, we both qualified as "city slickers" but would gain a lifetime of experience on horses under a variety of conditions before we left those hills.

Day three dawned clear, cool and bright. We eagerly packed the horses with enough gear and grub to last us 10 days. We were going elk hunting! Our destination that first morning was a spike camp that was a four-hour ride from base camp, nicknamed, appropriately enough, "Elk Camp." It was to be home for the next two or three days before we were scheduled to move higher up the drainage.

After setting up camp, Perry and I pulled out our spotting scopes and scoured the hillsides above us. The country quickly revealed itself as the elk haven we'd heard about. Small clusters of elk fed placidly in nearly every open basin we could see from our vantage point. Most were comprised of a mature bull with a harem of 10 to 20 cows, and the familiar ring of challenging bulls echoed from every direction. I slept fitfully that night in keen anticipation of what the morning would bring.

By 7:00 AM we'd mounted our horses and were working our way up from the valley floor. The golden-red mantled hue of the alder in the lower reaches transitioned to the cool of the spruce. The horses laboured up the steep slopes, finally bringing us to the lower edge of the open hilltops. We tied off our mounts and continued higher on foot, walking cautiously along the ridge top, careful not to skyline ourselves and reveal our presence to elk that might be watching from the safety of the timber. We slowly worked our way up the highest peak, stopping occasionally to glass the valleys below. The last few yards we belly-crawled, before peering over the top into the adjacent canyon. Immediately, we saw elk, though far enough away that we didn't have to conceal our location. We pulled the spotting scopes out of our packs and thoroughly glassed the herd, making out roughly 40 head grazing and milling about on an open slope nearly a mile away. Although there were a couple of decent bulls in the herd, none were worthy of making the long stalk across broken terrain, especially given the number of other elk we knew to be in the area.

After a quick swill from our water bottles, the three of us edged our way to the north slope of the peak, about 200 metres distant, and carefully peeked over the top before instantly ducking back behind cover. Four hundred metres below us and across the small coulee was a herd of more than 30 elk! In that first, quick glance we'd noticed at least four bulls, one of which was clearly a shooter. A team huddle reinforced that we were in agreement with a strategy. Perry would remain where we now cowered, while Robert and I would work our way back down the slope in hopes of closing the distance to about 200 metres. Careful to stay concealed, we inched our way down the open slope to a small rock outcropping and slowly peeked over.

The elk were oblivious to our presence, grazing peacefully along the edge of a thick stand of spruce. The bulls were cautious, as they usually are, and remained concealed in the dog-hair timber. We studied them through binoculars and simultaneously picked out the herd bull, confirming his status as a keeper. I pulled my rifle up and rammed a cartridge home, then settled down to find a comfortable shooting position and rest. As I snuggled in behind my scope, what had been an almost indiscernible background drone became suddenly louder. I sprang up to see what the commotion was, then instinctively ducked as an airplane barrelled through the canyon, a mere hundred metres above us and between where we sat dumbfounded and where the elk stood. Or rather were standing, as they were even less appreciative of the interruption than we were and immediately crashed through the trees and out of sight. The last we saw, the herd was crossing a ridge 600 metres away and disappearing into the next canyon.

"What the hell was that?!" I loudly inquired.

"That, my friend, was the local outfitter," Robert replied. "His camp's not far from here, and he's likely on his way in with hunters or gear. Timing is everything, I guess."

As the plane disappeared over the ridge, we regrouped to evaluate the situation and discuss strategy.

"Well," Robert led, "I don't think those elk have gone far. There's a second ridge they like to bed on about a mile past the one they crossed. Let's head there."

While a mile may not be far in other terrain, it was no mean feat from where we were. But our only option was to suck it up and start climbing ridges, so that's what we did.

Two hours later we stood 100 meters below the peak of another ridgeline. We'd heard the now-familiar bugle of a bull in the next valley and suspected these were the ones we were after. Robert and I slowly and carefully made our way to the top, conscious of not skylining ourselves and alerting the surely vigilant herd below. The last 20 metres were on hands and knees, and when we reached the edge, we peered over. Below us, scattered through the trees nearly 400 metres away, was our herd of elk. We counted nearly 40 head, predominantly cows and calves, with three or four bulls. We couldn't find the herd bull; however, and set up the spotting scope to more closely scrutinize the group. Scanning the trees carefully, we identified each and every animal. We counted three bulls, a 3x3 and two 4-pointers, but we knew the herd bull had to be there somewhere. So we started at the beginning again, glassing every inch of the treeline.

"There he is, Robert!" I whispered excitedly.

"Where? I don't see him."

"Look about halfway down the ridge in the middle of the herd. He's standing facing us with just the tip of his antlers extending past that big spruce."

Robert locked in on the bull and confirmed him to be the one we were looking for. I quickly set up the bipod on my rifle and snuggled in behind the scope, dialling the 3x-9x Bausch and Lomb up to 9 power. I was going to need all the help I could get if I was going to make this shot.

The elk knew, in their inimitable way, that something was up. A few cows started to make their way nervously to the ridgetop, staring intently in our direction. They couldn't have seen us, yet instinct told them we were there. I stayed on the bull and watched as he wandered aimlessly in a small circle, taking the time to bluff-charge a smaller bull that had gotten too close for comfort. I estimated his distance to be about 360 metres in the trees and below me at about a 45-degree angle. We couldn't move without exposing ourselves; if I was going to get him, it would have to be from there.

We'd been in place about 15 minutes, and Robert was beginning to get as antsy and impatient as the elk. But I'd already decided that I wouldn't shoot until I was comfortable and confident I could make the shot. The big bull continued his stroll through the trees, seemingly unaware of what was going on around him. Finally, he stopped and lifted his nose to the wind, checking the air for the welcoming scent of cows in heat. He stood quartered slightly away from me, with his entire body, except his near-side hind quarter, exposed. I knew it was now or never, and with no further hesitation, I squeezed the trigger. At the explosion, elk ran in every conceivable direction.

"Watch for the bull, Robert!" I exclaimed. Some of the elk scrambled down the ridge through the trees, others went up and over the ridge and still others went straight away, paralleling the ridge until they were out of sight in the dark timber.

"I didn't see him leave, Robert. Did you?"

"No," he replied, "but I'd already lost him in the trees from my vantage point before you shot. I wasn't sure where he was."

I returned my gaze to where I thought the bull had been standing and tried to identify it to Robert, and to Perry, who'd scrambled to the ridge top to join us at the sound of the shot.

"He was standing just beside the big spruce that's immediately below that stand of three pines. See the one with the funny, crooked top?"

"I got it," replied Perry.

"Well, look," I advised, "I'm going to walk down the ridge spine. When I get to the point above where the bull was last standing, wave to me."

With that, I started down the spine, anxious to see if my elk was down in the timber, or if he'd spit out the side somewhere and escaped. I kept looking back as I walked, sure I'd gone far enough, but the boys kept waving me forward. Finally, they signalled to stop, and I headed down off the ridge and into the thick conifer forest below. Deadfall littered the floor of the side slope, and I slowly worked my way through the chicane, keeping one eye to the ground out of respect for my knees while the other scanned the uneven terrain ahead, hoping to pick up the glint of an antler or the familiar tan colour that would betray the presence of a fallen elk.

Stepping over yet another downed tree trunk, my eyes immediately focused a mere six metres away. There was my prize, down where he'd been standing, and I let out a whoop that my companions could hear easily from high up on the ridge peak. He was a mature 5x5 with longer than average tines and average girth. He would later prove to be 5½ years old and score in the high 280s, not big by some elk standards, but a respectable bull for northeastern BC, which is renowned for its numbers of elk, not necessarily their size.

While Robert hiked back to get the horses, Perry and I set about the task of cleaning and quartering the elk. Two hours later Robert reappeared, leading two horses. We wrapped, packed and loaded the bull, then started the long trek back to camp. I developed a whole new respect for horses that day and still shudder at the thought of what the return trip to camp would have been like without the benefit of equine assistance.

We arrived back at the tent around 10:30 PM, exhausted but satisfied. A quick hot meal and a pot of coffee later we were all fast asleep, awaking early the next morning with renewed vigour. Our plan was to clean up camp and hang my elk, as the following day we'd be riding farther up the drainage to another spike camp in the hopes of finding a good elk for Perry. Together we suspended a hefty log between two large trees, four metres above the ground. I tied a cheesecloth bag holding the backstraps and tenderloin in the centre of the cross-pole, with a front and hind quarter firmly roped alongside, one on each side. The cape, antlers and skull we strapped high onto one of the supporting trees.

The following five days in the headwaters of the Gathto Creek were chockfull of adventure and misadventure alike. We got lost one night in the pitch dark; at midnight we had horses running every which way through the trees and mutiny on the minds of the riders. Fortunately, once we gave the horses their heads, we eventually found camp in a blinding snowstorm. Another morning, while riding up a steep, snow-covered slope, Perry completed a full backwards somersault while mounted on the back of his pony. How neither Perry nor the horse emerged any worse for wear amazes me to this day, but their acrobatic roll earned 10s across the board from the judges. On the positive side of the ledger, we had the inspiring opportunity to watch nearly 700 head of elk, some 30 moose (including a "herd" of 17, an honest 65-inch monster and one decent bull we watched stride over a high ridge nearly a thousand vertical feet above treeline), a handful of caribou and about 50 stone sheep. I accompanied Robert one day as he filled his resident sheep tag, taking a 12-year-old stone ram that threw itself off a ridge top, landing on its roof on the scree slope 50 metres below.

Perry played cat and mouse with a nice bull for two days, calling back and forth, before connecting early one afternoon after fooling him with a series of cow calls. He was a mature 6x5, scoring almost identical to the one I'd taken earlier. Tagged out, we were satisfied in knowing that we'd managed to collect the two largest elk we'd seen.

The return trip to Elk Camp, though largely a happy occasion, was not uneventful, featuring numerous horse wrecks as our pack train struggled its way home over the difficult terrain. Eventually, we neared camp, and my first thoughts turned to my elk and how it had fared in the days without me. My heart soon fell, for as we drew nearer and could see the hanging tree, no elk carcass was evident. Closer investigation revealed that while we'd been away, a black bear had visited camp. Climbing both support trees, he'd managed to reach out, tear down and haul away both front quarters, both hind quarters, the cape and skull. All that remained, swinging lonely and aimlessly in the cool breeze, was the bag containing the backstraps and tenderloins, either out of reach or simply not worth the effort for the certainly well-fed bruin. I didn't know whether to laugh or cry. Not only had I lost my trophy, I didn't have much of the prized meat to show for my efforts.

It was a discouraged group that unpacked and hit the hay that night. Morning light found us tracking the bear's getaway route. The trail was fairly obvious, littered as it was with the gleaming white, cleaned bones of my elk. Not far down the trail we found the cape and antlers, none the worse for their ground-excavating drag in the jaws of their abductor. That made me feel a little better, but I was still mourning the loss of the meat as we headed the last three hours down the trail to base camp. Rounding the final curve, it was obvious that there was more than one hungry and mischievous bear in the country. The kitchen at base camp was totalled; the walls were torn off their supporting frame, and the contents strewn across the site. Although lots of the food and gear bore the bear's signature tooth marks, the only real victim was a 25-kilo bag of sugar that had been reduced to mere shreds of burlap.

Our 12-hour drive home allowed plenty of time for Perry and I to relive and analyze our 12 days afield. Our bodies, minds and egos had been bruised and battered, but we wore the pain like medals, with two trophy capes and antlers, and an elk and an eighth worth of prime meat loaded in the camper behind us. We came to the conclusion that while Muskwa country may rightfully deserve its reputation as a pristine, wildlife-rich wilderness, getting in and out with your game just ain't that easy!

8

DANGER BAY: HUNTING GEESE IN THE LAND OF NANOOK

I'd heard and read about Kaska Goose Lodge long before I had the opportunity to visit. It's a legendary destination for water-fowlers because of the mind-boggling numbers of uneducated geese that funnel through the region on their way south each fall from their Arctic nesting grounds. Throw in the advantage of having a helicopter on standby in case the birds aren't staging close to camp, the nervous excitement of potential polar bear encounters, a gin-clear brook trout river on the lodge's doorstep and dizzying nightly displays of northern lights, and you have all the ingredients for a highly memorable experience.

"Uh, be a little careful if you leave the blind to retrieve a cripple. There's always a chance that a polar bear might beat you to it." This was clearly not going to be your typical goose hunt.

Kaska Goose Lodge owner Randy Duvell offered that subtle warning only half in jest. When you are hunting the Hudson Bay Lowlands in September, polar bears are as much a part of the landscape as the tens of thousands of geese migrating south from their High Arctic nesting grounds. In fact, over three days of hunting on Manitoba's Kaskattama River delta, I saw nearly 50 of the great white bears.

Collecting birds from across the eastern and central Arctic, the Hudson Bay Lowlands can best be described as one vast wetland complex paralleling the Hudson Bay coastline. Extending from western Québec to eastern Manitoba, the vast array of rivers, lakes, bogs and fens create a rather harsh and unforgiving landscape for humans. For a diverse array of fish, wildlife and birds, however, the region offers a productive and life-assuring refuge. This is especially the case for the abundance of migrating Canada, snow and Ross's geese that congregate in the region, making it a must-go destination for adventure-seeking waterfowlers. And recently, I finally had the chance to check it out for myself.

I'm always amazed at the ingenuity and effort dedicated individuals will invest in turning a relatively inhospitable place into something that goes well beyond providing basic creature comforts. Such is the case with Kaska Goose Lodge on Cape Tatnam, near the mouth of the Kaskattama.

My first morning started at 5:00 AM, as would each of the following mornings, with Randy dropping off a wake-up thermos of hot coffee and the day's weather forecast. After a quick but hot shower, I headed to the main lodge for a hearty breakfast, which included a steaming bowl of Manitoba's famous Red River cereal. And with that we were loaded into an Argo to begin the day's hunt.

The backdrop for hunting Kaska is unlike that of any other goose hunt I've experienced. The Argo paraded us through a melting pot of taiga, boreal and coastal lowland ecotypes, with the vegetation dominated by scrub spruce, Arctic willows, blueberries and various shrubs and sedges. Above the ATV's purr, I could hear the roar of waves breaking onto the Hudson Bay coast less than 500 metres distant. As we reached our blinds, the sun slowly lifted above the eastern horizon, and a new sound began to mix with the crashing surf—the unmistakable squeaks and squawks of restless snow geese. Then we saw them, skein after skein of birds trading against the azure sky. This was goose country like no other.

My hunting partner for the day was Lisa Ballard, a gifted writer and congenial outdoor television personality from Montana. Our blind was dug down into an esker and fortified with driftwood and spruce boughs; there was simply no way the geese, even notoriously suspicious snow geese, would be able to pick us out. But with little wind, the four dozen decoys we'd set around us and on the salt flat below appeared discouragingly listless.

It wasn't too long; however, before the first flight of birds, a cluster of eight Canadas, veered in to inspect the spread. As they crossed in front of us, on the outer edge of shooting range, Lisa and I rose in unison to swing. Two birds crumpled to our volley. Several subspecies of Canada geese pass through the region each fall, and our reward was a genuine odd couple—a giant Canada along with a Richardson's goose, one of the smaller of the recognized subspecies.

Even at a goose collection point such as the Kaskattama delta, the shooting can be slow on some days, and this turned out to be one of those days. With little wind, there were few new birds arriving from the north and east. And while there were literally thousands of birds already in the region, they were barely moving by mid-morning. Unlike across the Prairies and other parts of southern Canada, where goose hunting is focused around agricultural crops, the Hudson Bay lowlands are relatively uniform on a broad scale, making it more challenging to determine exactly where the birds want to be. When they're active and moving, decoys will bring them in; on quiet days, they don't appear to seek any specific location.

After a couple of hours, and with few birds flying, Lisa and I walked down to investigate the Hudson Bay shore. The world's second-largest inland sea is vast, cold and unforgiving with few signs that anyone had ever visited this stretch of shoreline before us. But the signs of the local wildlife were plentiful and obvious—myriad tracks of geese and other birds cross-hatching the sand, the straight-line depressions of caribou hooves and depressions dug into the sand ridges by polar bears seeking to cool themselves under the late-summer sun.

So, about the polar bears...Beyond serving as a natural funnel for migrating geese, northern Manitoba's Kaskattama River delta has also evolved as a collection point for the great white bears. They assemble here each year awaiting the formation of ice on Hudson Bay, which will allow them to hunt seals throughout the winter months. These are Canada's largest and most awe-inspiring predators, and even the sign of recent bear activity can send a cold shiver down your spine.

According to Randy, it's not unusual for the giant bears to wander through his camp, situated on the western bank of the Kaskattama. Fortunately, he observed that there has never been any serious conflict during the short September hunting window.

"They're generally pretty passive at this time of year," he says, "although you can never take them for granted and should always be cautious when you're wandering about."

Lisa and I eventually strolled back to our blind where, between bites of our bag lunches, we dropped a couple of beautiful and finely formed Ross's geese, the smallest of our goose species. These ivory-plumed birds aren't much bigger than a fat, grain-fed mallard. Without a meaningful breeze, however, the birds just weren't cooperating. So, with the arrival of the Argo to check on our progress, we packed up our decoys, collected fellow hunters Shel Zolkewich and Ron Peach from their blind a kilometre away and headed in.

It would have been easy to lament a disappointing day's goose hunt, but there was little point, especially with the prospect of catching sea-run brook trout heading up the Kaskattama on their annual spawning run. We all quickly shucked our waterfowling gear, grabbed our fishing tackle and hiked the few hundred yards from camp to the river's edge.

Just as you need a little wind to maximize goose hunting, you need low, clear water for optimal brookie fishing. In keeping with the spirit of the day, the river was high and silted. Timing is everything to outdoorsmen, making "you should have been here last week" a common refrain.

Still, you don't make the sale if you don't make the call, so with unbridled optimism we began casting.

With my 6-weight rod, I repeatedly cast out a pink conehead leech pattern, letting it swing down and across through any likely looking water. Before long, I had my first fish, a nice 18-inch trout, still a little pale, and not yet in the fully resplendent spawning colours it would soon sport.

The Kaskattama has an outstanding reputation for giving up trophy-sized fish, and I was hoping to hit the 20-inch mark, qualifying me for Master Angler status under Manitoba's popular fishing program. It was not to be; my biggest that afternoon was a 19-inch male. Still, despite less than ideal conditions, I was thrilled with the chance to fish for wild, native brook trout, which I consider to be Canada's most beautiful fish.

At one point while we fished, a large boar black bear stepped out of the forest and onto the riverbank just 100 metres upstream. If he noticed us, he certainly showed little concern and eventually slipped back into the dark cover of the trees. I guess you have to be a pretty tough black bear to live in such proximity to polar bears; there's no question which one would prevail if they ran into one another.

Starting the next morning, the north wind picked up, the temperature dropped and restless geese began to fly more predictably. That morning I partnered with Ron Peach, an outdoor writer from Kansas City, Missouri, setting up on a willow flat about five kilometres northwest of camp.

Our spread consisted of 20 silhouette snow goose decoys, a dozen snow windsocks and a half-dozen Canada shells. It was a relatively small layout by southern goose hunting standards, but more than enough where the geese are relatively uneducated and there's no meaningful competition. Our blind, meanwhile, reminded me of the standard prairie blind of years past—two chairs surrounded by a rectangle of cut willow limbs.

In little time, Ron and I had our limit of 16 Canadas, on this day all small birds. The gusts made shooting a challenge, as the geese turned quickly on the wind if they noticed anything suspicious on final approach, but in the target-rich environment, Ron and I had more than enough opportunity to settle it all rather quickly.

The snows were decidedly more cautious, but we made them pay whenever they committed, collecting a pair of the tiny Ross's along with a handful of blue geese. Blues are simply a colour phase of snow geese, but with their distinctive dark bodies capped by a white head, you can't help but target them when they arrive in a flock mixed with all-white birds. "Eagle heads" is the colloquial term many hunters use to describe them.

As we waited for more snows to arrive, Ron and I watched flock after flock of Canada geese land amid the decoys and around our blind. With our limit in hand we just sat back, slurped hot coffee from our thermoses and enjoyed the subarctic spectacle.

Our last day of hunting kicked off with Shel Zolkewich and I sharing a permanent blind along the river just north of camp, while Ron and Lisa shared a similar set-up some 300 metres to the south. All of us enjoyed our fair share of shooting, but we held back a little, having been given a little insight into the afternoon plans.

After wolfing down lunch at camp, Randy treated our group to one of the unique experiences that makes Kaska

Goose Camp stand out from all the others—a helicopter jaunt to fresh hunting grounds. We climbed into the Bell Long Ranger II that stands ever-ready to take hunters to wherever the birds may be staging along the countless miles of coastline, and flew 20 minutes to the east. Along the way, we saw moose and caribou going about their business in the truly remote landscape, free from human interaction. And, of course, we saw polar bears, including a large boar sprawled out along the shore less than two kilometres from where the chopper dropped us off to hunt.

We quickly set up the decoys we'd toted along and scrambled into a blind. Birds were cross-stitching their way over the salt flats in every direction, which made for challenging spotting, as you never knew from which direction the geese might arrive. Several times, in fact, we were caught totally off-guard, and inevitably a handful of geese would scoot unscathed through the decoys. It was just that busy.

Whenever I ventured out to retrieve a downed bird, especially if it had sailed a little before dropping, I'd invariably come across the generations-old caribou trails, as well as polar bear footprints. There were enough of the latter to keep me extra-vigilant during the retrieve; head-down hustling was not a prudent option. Fortunately, I didn't encounter a bear while collecting birds, and we shot a nice mixed bag of Ross's, snows, blues and Canadas, a fitting climax to the Kaska hunting experience.

As a final treat after dropping our hunting gear and birds back at camp, we took another short exploratory helicopter ride. First, we travelled south of camp to view the remnants of another time, the foundations of buildings constructed decades earlier by the Hudson's Bay Company in support of the fur trade. Then we headed northwest along the bay, spotting ducks, geese and cranes as we flew over the flats below.

Eventually, about 15 kilometres from camp, we came across a veritable El Dorado of polar bears, a stretch of shoreline with no fewer than 40 of the magnificent white creatures, some standing about, others sprawled atop the sand and still more dug into their sand caves. From big, mature boars to sows with cubs, a full cross-section of polar bears was represented. It was one of those sights you had to see to believe, and I still ask myself whether it was real or fantasy.

On that last evening, long after most of the others had gone to bed, I stood out on the deck of our cabin, watching the northern lights dance across the sky, a shimmer of emerald on a coal-black canvas, and reflected on my time at Kaska. Geese galore. Wild brook trout. Polar bears. And now, the *Aurora borealis*. All in all, the quintessential northern Canadian sporting adventure.

9

THE WORLD'S BEST BROOK TROUT RIVER, REALLY?

Through my early 20s I was an avid canoe tripper and paddled several rivers in Alberta and in the Yukon. Unfortunately,
I broke my back in a skydiving accident, and canoeing was
one of the long-term casualties of that mishap; for a long time
my lower back just couldn't handle the unsupported stress of
long paddles very well. I missed those trips considerably, so
when the opportunity to paddle and fish the Sutton River for
nine days presented itself, I was more than ready to jump
back into a canoe. And with Dave Kay as my partner and
a river full of fat brook trout, this truly remote fishing trip was
just what the doctor ordered.

It's well documented that anglers are, by nature, liars. Prevaricators might be a better term in these politically correct times. Either way, it's little wonder that it was with jaundiced eyes that I read the revised 2002 edition of Nick Karas' *Brook Trout*, or more specifically, the new chapter he entitled "The World's Best Brook Trout River."

Really? *The* best brook trout river in the world? That's quite a bold statement, although I suppose not an unusual one for a fisherman, let alone a fisherman who was by vocation a storyteller. Still, the description of the river seemed to ring true, and Karas was, after all, widely regarded as—dare I say it?—one of the world's most knowledgeable brook trout anglers.

And so it was that I took more notice than I might have otherwise when I saw a promotion for fly-in trips to northern Ontario's Sutton River. Or should I say *the* Sutton, the very river Karas described in his new chapter when he complained, "Our biggest difficulty was finding small fish for the frying pan."

Right away I knew there was just one thing to do, see for myself if Karas' claims were true. And I knew in a flash who I'd ask to come along. Dave Kay and I have shared more than a few angling and hunting adventures over the years, and the Sutton's remote wilderness setting would be right up his alley.

Getting to the Sutton is a logistical challenge. From my home in Edmonton, it meant a flight to Toronto followed by another flight north to Timmins. There we bought groceries and stayed overnight in a local motel, then rented a car for the three-hour drive farther north to Hearst. From there, it was another couple of hours by float plane via Hearst Air to Hawley Lake, the Sutton's headwaters.

The Sutton is not a particularly challenging river to navigate once you get there; it's just a helluva long way from civilization. Sliding languidly into Hudson Bay on the west side of James Bay, it's a mere 130 kilometres long, and most who paddle its length cover the distance in an easy 6 to 10 days, depending on how they want to split their time between paddling and fishing. Dave and I planned for nine days in all.

Albert Chookomoolin, a Cree born in 1949 in a mud hut at Hawley Lake, is the Sutton's unofficial river keeper. He still lives on the river with his wife and two sons, and guides anglers by way of a motorized canoe, taking them downstream a short distance to one of his tent camps, where they overnight. Other than that, Albert's clients don't see much of the river. But then, they're there to catch fish and, as we were to learn, you can wear out your best rod and reel on big brook trout in the Sutton's first 15 or so kilometres.

Dave and I planned instead to see it all, paddling the entire river by ourselves. Albert stores canoes for Hearst Air, and after picking one out of the mix and carefully loading our tent, grub, fishing gear and other necessities, we shoved off. After day two, when we passed Albert's tent camp, we wouldn't see another soul until we met our float plane at Hudson Bay. Mission creep was not an option. Once we were headed downstream, we had no choice but to make it to the pickup point on time.

On any canoe trip, the tendency is to make some miles the first day, loosening unused muscles and getting in sync with your paddling partner. But for Dave and me, an hour of cruising over pools teeming with colourful, fat brook trout was about 59 minutes more than we could stand. We soon stopped and quickly began casting flies over likely looking runs.

In short order we'd each hooked and landed several brookies up to 21 inches long. Like anxious football players, anglers can't relax until they get that first hit out of the way, and our initial stop did the trick. We cast knowing smiles at one another; if this was a harbinger of what lay ahead, the trip would definitely be one to remember.

Brook trout are the old souls of Canada's gamefish. They just want to be left alone, and if they could talk, I'm sure they'd cuss at every angler in turn, telling them to get the hell off their property. And unlike some of their trout and char brethren, brook trout aren't newcomer immigrants from abroad, and most don't venture on sea cruises only to come back fat and lazy.

No, brookies are working fish, doing what they've done in solitude for millennia, long before the first Indigenous people dangled a grasshopper on a bone hook in front of them. And lest we forget, they are arguably the most beautiful fish on our good earth.

Unfortunately, the distribution and average size of the species have diminished throughout most of its range because of development and fishing pressure. On the remote Sutton, however, brook trout can still reach their full potential in terms of numbers and size, and Dave and I aimed to take full advantage of that.

Over the days, we settled into an easy routine. We woke whenever we felt like it, brewed some fresh java over a fire, then waded lazily up and down the river as the mood struck us, casting as we went. If it's true that the greatest gift one fly-fisherman can bestow upon another is to walk 100 metres in the opposite direction, then it was Christmas every day on the Sutton. We both revelled in the solitude of a few hours alone on the wild pristine river crammed with hefty, eager trout. Catching fish was never a problem, and we quickly gave up counting those brought to the net.

Dave and I both enjoy the lore and legend described in historic brook trout literature, so we'd come well stocked with classic, glamorous brookie flies, determined to fish the river the traditional way. My fly wallet was crammed with time-tested Montreals, Trout Fins, Colonel Fullers and, of course, venerable Parmachene Belles. Well, I'm here to tell you that Sutton brook trout aren't the urban dandies of the Beaverkill River and similar streams in the Catskills and Adirondacks that have garnered so much press over the years. These fish wanted no part of anything dainty.

Despite making hundreds of casts, I managed to hook only one trout swinging my classic wet flies down and across. Talk about taking a knife to a gun fight. But every time I tied on a big streamer, a scrum of broad-shouldered squaretails chased it down like greyhounds on a mechanical rabbit. And, as it turned out, the bigger and rougher the fly, the better, with top choices including Bow River Buggers and Muddler Minnows. When the streamers wore out their welcome, skittering a chunky floating mouse pattern across the surface was sure to elicit a strike.

Around noon each day, we'd wander back to camp, enjoy a quick lunch, pull up stakes and paddle until mid-afternoon before choosing our next campsite. We'd then fish through the late afternoon and early evening, keeping a couple of trout for dinner. Dave is a cook of no insignificant talents, and every night he crafted meals befitting the grandest restaurants.

I knew my place and was quite content to handle cleanup chores, knowing full well I was reaping the better part of the deal. For when Dave wasn't baking teriyaki-style fillets or frying fish in a ponzu-onion sauce, he was picking wild berries and making his own black currant jam. We might have been sleeping on the ground floor, but thanks to Dave, we were dining in the penthouse every night.

When you're paddling and fishing the days away and sleeping in a tent every night, the weather takes on more significance than it would at home. Our first four days on the water saw clear blue skies, no wind and a sweltering sun, perfect conditions for a wilderness fishing trip some might suggest. But warm weather comes at a cost in these parts, with mosquitoes and blackflies emerging in droves and turning each day into a battle of physical and mental endurance. Fortunately, the grey, overcast and drizzly skies and cool air that greeted us through most of the latter half of the trip offered a welcome respite.

Most importantly, the eager fish didn't seem to care one way or the other about the weather.

In many respects, the Sutton is an innocuous, if deceptive, river. In most places it's 60 to 100 metres wide and relatively flat. There's no white water to speak of, though the boulder gardens are numerous, and late-season paddlers need to be wary of shallow sections. Although some pools could hide a semi-trailer, you can ford the river on foot across most runs. The banks are generally abrupt, and willows line much of the shoreline, placing decent camping spots at a premium. Miss one, and it can be several kilometres until the next suitable spot appears.

Shrouding the willows is an array of drunken spruce and tamarack, leading you to believe the river cuts through a vast tract of boreal forest. It's all smoke and mirrors; however, as the trees only extend back 100 metres or so before giving way to flat, relatively featureless tundra. The first time you hike from the river to the tundra, you quickly become aware you're well into northern Canada, a stark reminder that creature comforts are a long, long way away. That you're also paddling through Polar Bear Provincial Park is another clue you're deep in the wilderness, and the reason you're always within spitting distance of a shotgun and slugs.

As I reflect on our days on the Sutton, I suppose I should be describing tales of bent rods and one massive hard-fighting fish or another or the cautious trout in the corner pool that took me eight different flies and two patient hours to fool. But the truth is, the fish were so plentiful and so darn big on average that the memory of one fades quickly into another. You simply can't separate one fish, one pool or even one day from another. And yet, you can't become jaded on the Sutton, because the experience is simply too incredible. There are few dips and valleys; it's all one big high.

To be fair, neither Dave nor I landed one of the seven-pound bruisers that swim these waters, as evidenced by the photos I've seen and the stories I've heard from others. But we caught enough wild halos in the three- to five-pound range to last several lifetimes, and I don't believe we caught two fish shorter than 16 inches over the entire nine days.

It was one of those adventures where you can only tell people, "You had to be there to believe it."

And as for Nick Karas? I can find no argument as to why the Sutton doesn't deserve his praise as the best brook trout river in the world.

10

FACE TO FACE WITH OLD EPHRAIM

A career change landed me in Fort St. John in northeastern BC, working for the provincial wildlife department. After many years of self-employment, I found the constraints of working in government to be challenging and moved back to Alberta after only a year. My time in BC did give me resident status; however, allowing me to hunt grizzly bears without requiring that I hire a guide. Of course, all that has changed. There is no longer a grizzly bear hunt in BC, and Alberta's season has also been closed for many years. The shame is that these decisions have been based largely on social pressures, not on sound science or sustainable wildlife management principles.

What should have been a relaxing and enjoyable ATV ride down the mountain turned out to be a nightmare. We had mistakenly assumed that going downhill would be as easy or at least easier than riding uphill. Wrong! With our machines heavily laden, piled high with gear and a remarkably heavy bear hide, the high centres of gravity we barely noticed heading up to camp became a virtual death sentence on the way down. Every turn in the trail or uneven stretch of ground resulted in the ATVs looking to swap ends with themselves. The trike I was riding was particularly bad; they're unstable by nature and with the compounding influence of a steep, uneven trail...well, let's just say I understand why they are no longer manufactured.

I took several spills on that bike, fighting gravity to retain control of the machine the whole way down the mountain. By the time I finally rounded the last curve before the road I was utterly exhausted, bleeding from numerous scrapes and cuts and clutching my chest in agony where a branch to the ribs had cushioned one of my falls. To top it off, I was now riding a bike with no handbrakes; both had been torn from the machine. Doug was in only slightly better shape. His machine, a four-wheeled quad, was significantly more stable, but he had bruised himself considerably helping me stabilize my trike in some of the trickier sections of the trail. It was well into night before we trailered the machines and climbed into the truck cab for our long journey home. Clearly, grizzly hunting brings with it more peril than the legendary unpredictability of the bears themselves.

We've got no elephants in North America; Simba doesn't patrol our prairies; you won't bump into Mbogo in an alder thicket; and there are no leopards lurking along the edges of our aspen forests. And finding a rhinoceros? Simply preposterous! No, but when you mention dangerous game to most hunters, their first thoughts typically turn to Africa and her vaunted "big five." But in the northwestern states and provinces, we have our own representative of the "ultimate game." The kind that fights back. The great bears of Alberta, BC, Alaska and the Territories may not carry with them the reputation that Africa's big game does, but don't let that fool you. For heart-stopping, in-your-face excitement, the grizzly bear takes a back seat to no one.

Like most North American hunters, I've long held the dream of hunting grizzlies. I can't explain it to a non-hunter, but if you're a hunter you know what I mean. I'm certainly not interested in their meat, though I've heard it can be quite delicious, especially in the fall. Their pelt, while gorgeous, making for a stunning rug or full body mount, isn't what draws me to them. No, it's the thrill of hunting something that is fully equipped and quite prepared in most circumstances to fight back that has made them so irresistible to me. It's the challenge, the adrenaline rushes and the fear that make the grizzly so compelling to hunt.

You say you're not afraid of grizzlies, that hunting or hiking in their backyard doesn't make the hair on the back of your neck stand up? You feel perfectly cool, calm and collected as long as you have your trusty .338 Win. Mag. at your side? I say you're either a fool or a liar; choose whichever you prefer. In either case, you should put away your guns and quit hunting. If a griz don't set your old ticker on high, there's no point in being out there. Old Ephraim, as the mountain men referred to him, is no tin god. He earned his stripes the old fashioned way, on the carcasses of those who found themselves toenail to toenail with him. The risk and the accompanying adrenaline rush is what has drawn me to him over the years.

So it went that year after year after year I applied for one of the few grizzly bear tags available in my home province of Alberta. I was even lucky enough to be drawn one year. But 10 days in the heart of the Chinchaga River valley didn't pan out. We saw no bears except a few blacks and not even a single grizzly track.

It was with obvious excitement then, that I accepted a full-time position in British Columbia, Canada's westernmost province and home to half the nation's grizzlies and 25 percent of the North American population. As a resident hunter I didn't need to apply for a tag. At the time, you could simply pick one up over the counter to hunt in some regions of the province.

It didn't take long to find a bear-hunting partner. I'd known Doug Russell since his days with Ducks Unlimited in Alberta. A year and a half before my move to BC, Doug had accepted a similar position in neighbouring Dawson Creek to the one I took in Fort St. John. He, too, was excited about the possibility of hunting the great "grizzled" bears, and we quickly started making plans.

Grizzly bears are like any other big game animal; the key to hunting them is finding suitable habitat. As my friend Bob Kress says, "If you want to pick apples, you have to go where the apple trees are." Doug and I started researching potential hunting areas. As we hadn't applied for a limited entry tag, we were restricted to the general open zones. Essentially, this meant one of the northern regions. Discussions with all who'd offer their free advice soon found us settled on an area in the province's northwest, off the Cassiar Highway. This region boasts a great diversity of habitats, from deeply incised river valleys to mid-elevation spruce/fir forests to high alpine meadows and rugged peaks of exposed rock. In short, every kind of terrain any self-respecting grizzly could want.

The area we'd selected was accessible by ATV, so a Sunday afternoon in early May found us loaded and on the road with a quad, a trike and a week's worth of camping gear and grub in tow. It was a 16-hour drive from home to our valley of choice, so we opted to pull over and catch a few winks on the roadside along the way. It was early afternoon on Monday before we swung off the highway, parked the truck and loaded up the ATVs for the climb into the headwaters of the valley.

The traverse up the side of the south-facing slope was relatively uneventful, though Doug and I each managed to roll our ATVs once. We were to find out later just how much more difficult it is to go downhill on heavily laden ATVs, especially on one of the three-wheeled variety, upon which I was precariously perched. Our path was a long-abandoned trail used by tree planters, and we followed it steadily for two and a half hours until it ended abruptly. There was no way to go any further; deadfall and slash made further progress on the machines impossible. In that case, we decided we had found the ideal campsite. With no further ado we set about erecting our week's accommodations, pitching our two-man tent. We found a small stream only 100 metres away, and after collecting some water, fixed ourselves a quick supper, built a small fire and sat back to evaluate the surrounding terrain and plan the next day's hunt. In short order we were both fast asleep.

As the first shards of morning light broke over the alpine peaks to the east, Doug and I finished a simple breakfast and stuffed the rest of our day's provisions into daypacks. We both agreed that we should climb to higher ground, primarily in an attempt to get a better look at the valley we'd be hunting over the next several days. Doug climbed up the first peak, drawn by what appeared to be one of the few open, south-facing grass slopes in the valley, a natural feeding site for bears in spring. I decided to stay along the creek bank, following it upstream toward its headwaters.

When I found the spot, I knew it immediately. I was standing at a textbook-perfect location for searching out bears. The creek bed was nearly 130 vertical metres below me. Directly below and across from me was an island in the creek that featured thick alder and willow shrubs within a natural mosaic of coniferous trees and open knolls. Immediately downstream of my position, a second feeder creek and the one I sat above fed into the primary watercourse. From my vantage point on the east-facing bank I could see a full 270 degrees. Anything travelling toward the natural funnel of the creek confluences would not escape my field of view. I settled in at the base of a tree in the lee of the wind to watch and wait. I've always tried to follow the same approach to spring bear hunting—put myself in quality habitat and wait. Spring bears move considerable distances in their quest for rich food sources. As the early season's sun melts away winter's insulating snows, the various plant communities green up in a yearly repeated order, depending predominantly on their respective elevation, aspect and moisture regime. The bears know their home ranges intimately and move in order to take advantage of the best foods as they emerge and green up. I've found it productive to identify these prime food sources and wait, knowing that bears will show up eventually.

Once settled, I pulled up my 10x42 binoculars and started to glass the surrounding terrain. My depth of field was not so great that I needed to use a spotting scope, and I find binoculars easier on the eyes when long bouts of glassing are required. I spent the bulk of that day peering into every nook and cranny visible from my lair. Although I saw no bears, I had confidence in the spot and planned to return. At about 4:00 pm I decided to head back to camp; Doug would be back, and I wanted to compare notes. I slowly worked my way back, in large part because of the labyrinth of deadfall that carpeted the forest floor. It made for continual slow walking and bruised shins.

Doug was waiting for my return and related that he hadn't had much better luck than I did. But we were just on day one; we had lots of time left. We agreed a hot supper was in order, so while I started a fire, Doug went to retrieve our food from where it hung on a snag about 100 metres from camp. He was back in short order, urgently encouraging me to follow.

"There's three grizzlies just over the creek bank! A sow and two cubs!" he cautioned.

We scampered back to the area of our food cache, and Doug pointed down the creek slope. Sure enough, a beautiful honey-blonde sow with two year-old cubs worked her way along a ridge, feeding as she went. The cubs followed as best they could but succumbed regularly to curious natural attractions before Ma urged them along with loving swats of her platter-sized paws. They were only 120 metres or so as the crow flies from our vantage point, but because of the prevailing winds they were completely unaware of our presence. We watched with fascination for about 15 minutes before the trio disappeared into the darkness of the trees.

We returned to the tent and our supper full of newly found excitement and confidence; we were now sure that we were in quality bear habitat. Better yet, we'd enjoyed the privilege of watching a family of mountain grizzlies interacting with one another in their native habitat, something only a fortunate few people ever experience. After a quick meal and dish duty, Doug retired to the tent for a brief rest while I handled the hunter's ritual of staring blankly into the licking flames of a dying fire. We'd planned to get organized in a half hour or so and head out together again for the last few hours of evening light.

I was lost in the fire's embers when a light coughing sound caught my attention. I turned to the tent to see Doug resting comfortably, immersed in a paperback novel, so I returned to the solitude of my fire vigil. I don't really know what caused me to look up again a few minutes later. Perhaps I'd heard another sound; perhaps it was sheer chance; or perhaps it was some primitive instinct come to the fore. In any case, I lifted my head and found myself staring straight into the intimidating eyes of a boar grizzly, his chocolate brown head framed perfectly by the handlebars of the two ATVs parked one behind the other, no more than 35 metres from where I sat.

Needless to say, I didn't stay sat for long. Working on pure instinct and adrenaline, I leapt to my feet, grabbed my .300 Win. Mag. from where I'd leaned it against a nearby tree and quickly racked a 180-grain Winchester Fail Safe into the chamber.

"Doug! Griz!" I said softly, but with enough urgency that Doug reacted instantly, scrambling out of the tent to where his rifle lay.

Meanwhile, the bear and I continued our staring contest, both of us unsure about what to do next. I couldn't really tell how big he was because all I could see was his head. From the distance between his ears, he looked to have a relatively large skull, but his body was completely hidden by the ATVs. In any case, I certainly didn't want to shoot this bear in the head unless his actions left me no other alternative. I'd realized from the start that his intentions, at least initially, were not aggressive. He'd walked into our camp with the wind at his back, following along a well-used game trail. I think he was as surprised by our sudden encounter as I was.

By this time, Doug had his rifle up and was moving to his left in an attempt to get a broadside view of the bear.

"He's a good one, Ken!" he shouted, confirming my suspicions.

At the shout the bear swung to his left and started running. Immediately, he was out of my view and into the brush. I turned and leapfrogged my way over the deadfall behind the tent to where I hoped I could catch a glimpse of him on the move. Just as I broke into a clearing I saw him; he'd slowed to a walk, quartering away from me at a distance of about 70 metres. I raised my rifle, picked my spot and squeezed the trigger. At the shot the grizzly immediately sprinted for the safety of the dense vegetation on the steep creek bank slopes, and before I could get off a second round, disappeared over the crest. Doug and I both trotted over, meeting at the top of the creek bank and hoping for a glimpse of the bear moving through the thick brush. But all was quiet; we saw no movement.

From the moment I first saw the bear until Doug and I met on the bank, I'd say that no more than 45 seconds had elapsed. We were both a little short of breath, in part because of our short runs over and around the deadfall to the bank, in part because we'd just come face-to-face with a boar grizzly on the doorstep of our two-man tent and in part because we both knew he'd been hit and was somewhere below us, likely holed up in an alder thicket awaiting our pursuit. We both felt he'd been hit good; Doug was sure from his vantage point that it had been a chest hit. He said he'd been just about to shoot as well when he heard the report of my .300 and saw the bear react. Doug had actually been in a position to shoot before I was but had held off in a gracious gesture to allow me first crack at the bear I'd "discovered."

We stood together deciding what to do next. The creek bank extended down on a 45-degree angle for about 600 metres ending at the creek bed. The slope was a dense thicket of alder and willow trees with a nearly impenetrable understory of forbs and shrubs. Somewhere in there was my bear, and there was a good chance that we'd find out just why "Old Ephraim" is considered by the vast majority of hunters to be the most dangerous of North America's big game.

There was no sign of blood at the place he'd gone over the bank, so Doug and I decided to work our way down the nearest ridge. It provided us some measure of elevation over the adjacent terrain and offered the easiest walking. We'd just started down when I spotted the dark outline and mass of brown fur at the base of a dense alder. He was breathing but down and unable to rise. Like mature bears are prone to do, he was facing his back trail, ready to meet head-on anyone who dared follow him. Fortunately, an anchoring shot ended the drama before it escalated. In the end, he fell little more than 100 metres from our tent door.

Because of the steep slope and dense vegetation, skinning him proved to be a much more difficult chore than we'd anticipated. He was too heavy to move easily on the uneven terrain, and including the time to take a few photos, it was nearly two hours later before we were settled back down around the campfire. It took several hot teas before we'd talked ourselves out and were ready to turn in for the night. It was only day one, and we'd already taken a grizzly on our back porch and had seen a sow with two cubs close enough to hit with a rock. We slept fitfully that night, all too aware that through some good fortune we'd taken a bear on our first full day of hunting but knowing, too, that we were now camped with a grizzly carcass, prime bear bait, only 100 metres from our flimsy accommodations.

We returned the next morning to the spot I'd found overlooking the creek confluence in the hopes of locating a bear for Doug. While I remained confident that this was the spot to be, Doug wasn't so sure. Doug stays very fit and likes to be on the move while hunting, and that approach has proven successful for him. After an hour or so of waiting and watching, Doug couldn't stand it any longer.

"I'm going to head back up to higher ground, I'd like to check that open grassy knoll again," he advised. I nodded my agreement, confirming that I'd sit tight in my perch. With that Doug headed into the bush and up the mountain while I huddled back down in an attempt to stay out of the biting wind.

It couldn't have been 20 minutes later that I saw HIM. He was an absolute brute, half again bigger than the mature boar I'd taken the day before. He sauntered and waddled into an opening on the island in the creek below me in the manner all truly big bears move. His thick chocolate fur rippled in the breeze as he moved slowly, feeding his way from opening to opening. I watched in awe for 10 minutes, unsure of what to do. I knew I had to get Doug's attention, and that meant I had to risk spooking the bear. With little choice, I pointed my rifle skyward and squeezed.

At the sound the big bear casually raised his head for a moment, then lowered it again and resumed feeding. Even though he was only a shade over 200 metres away, my advantage in elevation and a favourable wind effectively concealed my location and proximity. All I could do now was sit and wait for Doug. There was no doubt that he'd come on the run; a rifle shot from a tagged-out hunter can mean only two things, that there's trouble or something of great interest.

As luck would have it, Doug arrived, breathless after a near death-defying run down the mountain through deadfall, no more than two minutes after the big grizzly boar had calmly ambled out of sight and into the dense timber of the creek bottom. After explaining the situation, we split up and worked our way along the creek bank in hopes of spotting the great bruin below us. To go down after him in the dense tangle of trees and shrubbery would have been fruitless.

As I stood glassing the banks, a crack of bush caught my attention, and I wheeled to the right. My eyes immediately locked on another pair of eyes! Unfortunately, they weren't Doug's, rather the coal-black eyes of a grizzly, cresting the creek bank in full flight. He was heading straight for me at a distance of about 40 metres.

I shouted a warning to Doug, who stood about 30 metres behind me, and instinctively raised my rifle. At the shout, however, the bear turned 90 degrees and ran past me, broadside and at full throttle, barely 25 metres away.

It was apparent that, despite our first impression, this bear was not running at us but was running from something. No doubt this grizzly, who appeared to be a three- or four-year-old bear, had bumped into the big guy himself and was informed in no uncertain terms to clear out or become an ursine sacrifice to the King of the Valley. It took a few minutes to settle my heart down to the level where I was getting the necessary amount of oxygen again to all parts of my body. Doug had passed on the shooting opportunity despite the short distance; a bear running through the trees is, at best, an iffy target. Besides, we were looking for the big boy I had seen earlier.

We searched the rest of that day and throughout the week without seeing another sign of that monstrous chocolate bear. Our experiences that one day convinced Doug; however, that sitting in wait over good habitat was a productive approach to bruin hunting. We sat over that creek confluence for most of the following three days without seeing a "shooter" bear. We were rewarded for our patience; however, when one afternoon a sow with three cubs appeared below us on the same island where I'd seen the big boar. We watched them for several hours, playing, nursing, feeding on the fresh spring shoots and sleeping, with mama bear and the three baby bears curled up together in a tight, furry ball. It was a truly wonderful and unique outdoor experience.

We pulled up camp late on Saturday, deciding that we could make it out to the road and our vehicle before dark. We were both tired, yet satisfied with what had been an exhilarating hunt. True to his form, Doug was just as excited for me having taken a grizzly as he would if he'd been the fortunate one.

Our week on bear mountain had been all a hunter could ask for, full of excitement and tempered with equal portions of good fortune, fun and terror. In total, we saw 11 different grizzly bears in five days of hunting. We experienced in that short time every weather pattern possible, from fog and snow, to rain and sleet, to gale-force winds. We even had a day of t-shirt weather—25 degrees and not a breath of wind.

My grizzly quest was all I'd longed for and more, experiencing several close encounters with the iconic bears. As such, I think I've satisfied my hunger for the bruin once and for all. I really was chasing the experience more than the bear and no longer have the passion that drove me for so many years. On the other hand, I've yet to hunt the massive coastal brown, or Kodiak, bear. I understand that they offer hunters a little excitement now and then, too!

11

A MOOSE HUNTER'S SNOWY LAMENT

If there's a more welcoming place anywhere in the world than Newfoundland, I've yet to find it. Before this trip I'd only visited The Rock on one occasion, and that was for business reasons that didn't allow me to explore beyond St. John's. But in the brief time I did spend there, I fell in love with the people and their attitude. Despite having struggled for many years as a result of declines in their economy, particularly the commercial fishing industry, I found Newfoundlanders to be steadfastly positive and optimistic, the kind of people you just can't get enough of. After that first visit I made a promise to myself to go back and discover just what it is they know that the rest of us don't. To do that, I'd have to get into the province's heartland.

Think of Newfoundland and what emerges are images of quaint seaside villages, gregarious hard-working people, raucous kitchen parties, lively folk music, rugged Atlantic coastlines, inclement weather that can erupt out of nowhere, and a rich and storied fishing culture. And if you're a hunter, moose.

Although moose are not native to the island, their story in the last century is one of spectacular growth. In 1878, a bull and cow were brought in from Nova Scotia and released near Gander Bay. Their fate is unclear. Then in 1904, two bulls and two cows from New Brunswick were introduced southeast of what is now Gros Morne National Park. By the 1920s, good numbers of moose were recorded more than 80 kilometres away; by 1935, the animals occupied much of the island, with the first moose sightings recorded on the Avalon Peninsula in 1941.

Currently, Newfoundland's moose population is estimated at 125,000 animals or roughly one moose for every four residents, giving The Rock what is widely considered the world's densest population of the giant ungulates. The largest member of the deer family is now as much a part of Newfoundland culture as the cod jig or the tin whistle.

Despite the numbers, the island's moose don't have the cachet of their relatives in Yukon or northern BC. They aren't as large-bodied, nor do they sport similarly enormous wingspans. So, in today's world of hunting, where size matters, Newfoundland moose don't get the respect they rightly deserve. Still, they've long been on my hunting bucket list. And considering that my long-time pal Brian Hagglund had never shot a moose, a trip to Newfoundland was going to be just the antidote both of us were seeking.

Or so we thought.

Our jumping off point was Portland Creek, two hours north of Corner Brook on Newfoundland's western shore. Leonard Payne, owner of Northern Peninsula Big Game Outfitters, loaded us onto his 1958 Beaver for the 35-minute flight southeast to Woody Lake, our base for the week-long hunt. Once at camp, we stowed our gear, wolfed down a quick breakfast, hopped into a boat with guides Larry Parsons and Tad Hynes, and motored across the small lake. From there, a half-hour hike up a rough-hewn trail through thick brush took us to a lookout point known affectionately as "the Tit."

The moose were well into their rut, so our primary tactic throughout the week was to gain the high ground from where we could glass the surrounding landscape, looking for bulls on the move. Once we found them, we'd try to call them into shooting range.

We stayed up top that first day for about seven hours. The surroundings reminded me of a tundra landscape—predominantly open country interspersed with small wetlands, copses of shrubs and trees, and rocky outcroppings. We spotted a cow and calf, a lone woodland caribou, and just before noon, a medium-sized bull walking a ridgeline about a mile and a half away.

Despite the distance, Tad cooed his best lovesick cow call. Almost immediately, the bull halted, turned and headed down the ridge toward us. Through binoculars we watched as it ambled through the chicane of rock and shrubs before it plunged into dense brush. We expected him to continue, anticipating he'd emerge from the trees about 300 metres from where we were perched. Twenty minutes later, however, there was no sign of him.

Perhaps he'd bumped into a receptive cow, or maybe his moose intuition had gotten the better of us. Whatever the case, we never saw the bull again. Still, our anticipation for the week was buoyed by how quickly he'd responded to our call. As the afternoon continued to unfold, the wind increased steadily, and by the time we clambered down to the boat, whitecaps covered the lake—an ominous harbinger of what lay ahead.

We were on the trail by 7:00 AM the following morning. An hour out from camp, we rested on a ridgeline that provided a commanding view of an immense valley. As we watched, a huge black bear lumbered across an opening providing an entertaining sideshow, his ebony fur shining in the early morning light. With no moose in sight, however, we carried on across the valley and up the other side.

The walking was tough, and it made me wonder how this land came to be known as The Rock. With much of the habitat wet and spongy, "The Bog" might have been a far more appropriate nickname. On we slogged, despite Brian's mumbling references about a "death march," and by 10:00 AM we'd settled down again to glass, this time overlooking a broad expanse of wet, open country interspersed with dense coniferous timber.

After just five minutes, Brian whispered excitedly, "Moose!"

Turning our attention to where he was pointing, we saw a young bull disappear into the trees about 350 metres away. Tad was quick to sound his call, and we waited patiently. The bull didn't respond, but we anticipated that he could be coming our way.

Fifteen minutes had passed when I caught sight of movement in a completely different direction. A second bull, likely having heard our call, was on the move 250 metres out and closing before he, too, evaporated into the trees. Right at that moment, the first bull reappeared 100 metres below us. Just his head, neck and shoulders were visible as he stood along the edge of a bush, cautiously scanning the area before stepping out.

Having won the rock-paper-scissors competition to determine who'd shoot first, I motioned for Brian to get ready. I wanted him to get a crack at his first moose. Brian didn't have to be asked twice. He quickly got on the shooting sticks, and when it felt right, hit the switch. Just like that, we had our first moose. And having watched the two bulls come to our call, we were certain the stories of Newfoundland's dense moose numbers were true.

Tad and Larry went to work dressing the young bull, their deft handling of the axe reminding me just how capable they were as outdoorsmen. In their hands, an axe is a multi-purpose tool, good for blazing trails while on the move, testing water depths and rendering a moose into precise, packable pieces in mere minutes.

After our moose was cut and packed for travel, we hung around for another hour, hoping the second bull would reappear. He never did show up, but before leaving we spotted a third bull more than a kilometre away. Like the others, he turned in response to our call, but once again something waylaid him and he never made it to within shooting distance of our lookout.

By the time we headed for camp, ominous grey clouds scudded across dark skies, rain began to fall and the wind picked up. Under heavy packs, the walk back was a struggle, especially with having to avoid ankle traps, many hidden beneath the carpet of soft vegetation. The safest-looking ground was as slippery as a politician, and even the caribou trails, well-worn after decades of use, weren't safe to use. Often we had to awkwardly straddle them to find firm footing. Still, we soldiered on in good spirits, reconfirming that there's no elixir quite like success when hunting.

With dawn the following morning, the bad weather had really moved in. Radio reports advised that the coast was experiencing sustained 100-kilometre winds and 10-metre seas, leading to ferry, airport and highway closures. Hurricane Ophelia, a Category 3 storm, had unexpectedly turned eastward and was skirting Newfoundland's shores. Inland, with the plummeting temperatures, the rain had turned to a Slurpee-like concoction of sleet and snow, pushed along by the ever-rising winds.

We assessed the situation and collectively agreed that conditions were still acceptable for hunting, so bright and early, we were in the boat and motoring across the rising swells on Woody Lake. Once across, a 20-minute walk took us to Larry Lake, so-named for our guide, and a waiting boat, which we were forced to row. Thirty minutes later we hit the far shore, beached our craft and started off on a precarious one-hour hike across the rolling landscape. In the worsening weather, the trails were slick. At one point, I completely lost my footing, hitting the ground in a sloppy heap.

Our destination was a small lake known locally as Highland Pond, and by the time we arrived, we were soaked to the skin. Huddling beneath some trees, we quickly built a fire to warm our shivering carcasses and dry out as best we could. By this time, the winds had picked up, gusting to 80 kilometres an hour, and the sleet and snow mixture was moving horizontally across the land, stinging our faces like a swarm of angry hornets. We hunkered down for an hour and a half before finally deciding the smart move was to high-tail it home. Not even the most amorous cow call would convince a bull to budge from shelter under these conditions.

As the storm intensified, with snow obliterating any vestige of the trail, our retreat was laboriously slow and cumbersome. We reached Larry Lake only to find a bubbling cauldron of whitecaps. Getting into the rowboat wasn't even a consideration, so we grimly continued walking. When we finally reached Woody Lake, the awaiting motorboat was filled to the gunnels with water—not that we would have launched into the gale-force winds and churning waters in any case. We had no choice but to put our heads down and slog it around the lake back to camp.

To protect ourselves from the stinging sleet, we trekked through the dense trees encircling the shoreline, slowly clambering over and around the deadfall that littered our route. By the time we reached camp, there was nearly a foot of snow on the ground and no sign of it letting up anytime soon.

That evening, after a hot supper had restored some semblance of comfort, we were brought to immediate attention by a resounding thump and an accompanying scream. A towering spruce had snapped in the fierce winds, crashing down on the cabin's roof directly above the camp cook's bedroom. Fortunately, only the top of the main stem had struck the roof, though the impact was heavy enough that the burners were knocked off the stove. Had the tree been any closer to the building, the full weight of the trunk would have undoubtedly broken through the ceiling, causing considerable damage and potential injury. We were all beginning to feel more than just a little worried that the storm would leave greater scars than those suffered by the cabin before it was finished with us.

The high winds and heavy snow continued through a fitful night, with dozens more trees pushed down. Fortunately, no others hit the cabin. With morning came the realization it would be a "snow day," meaning no hunting, a rare occurrence for the first week of October in Newfoundland.

The next day, the temperatures dropped to well below freezing, but the wind and snow had eased somewhat. Suffering cabin fever, we ventured out a kilometre or so to hunt, but it was fruitless. We didn't see so much as a single track in the half-metre of snow, evidence that the moose were no longer on the move, although you couldn't blame them given the conditions.

Walking was treacherous, too, because of the hazardous flashets that pockmarked the area currently concealed beneath the snow. These pools, while generally less than three metres in diameter, can be just as deep as they are wide, and stepping into one under these conditions would be disastrous and potentially fatal.

Little changed over the next two days; the cold wind blew strong and the snow-and-sleet slurry continued to fall. We'd venture out occasionally on short forays but didn't cut even a single moose track. Our hunt was officially at an end, and all we could do was wait until the weather let up enough to allow a float plane to fly in for us. Fortunately, we were rewarded with a tasty young bull to take home for the freezer and had discovered for ourselves that Newfoundland's moose were as plentiful as advertised. Not so fortunate, however, the province's reputation for unpredictable weather was equally valid. In all, we spent seven days in camp, with only two real days of moose hunting.

But we'd go back in a heartbeat.

12

THE LAKE OF ENDLESS OPPORTUNITIES

Despite living only a two-hour drive away for three years, in that time I didn't spend so much as a single day at Lake of the Woods. The best that I could claim was having stared vacantly out a car window at the vast lake, for decades a revered summer playground for countless vacationing Canadians and Americans. I was a teen at that time and had other priorities on my adolescent mind. Years later, when I was invited to report on the area's fishing and hunting on assignment with *Outdoor Canada* magazine, I took along Dave Kay, who I knew to have a passion for Canada's Shield country. As it turns out, he was so enamoured with the region he's been returning with his family every year since. When diversity of opportunity is the measuring stick, the region certainly must rank as one of Canada's foremost hunting and angling destinations.

L ong before dawn, the stars twinkled for us alone. Huddled in the boat with my back to the wind, the silhouette skeletons of late-season trees slipped past on both sides as Stephen Hanson guided us through the warren of points and islands. With Lake of the Woods' diversity of shoreline gradients and multitude of prop-eating submerged reefs, I would have had to pick my way carefully even under the brightest midday sun. Stephen, however, never once eased up on the throttle, his understanding of the safest passages undoubtedly born of the knowledge that only experience can provide. Rounding one more rocky point shrouded in the remnants of the season's wild rice crop, Stephen expertly let off on the throttle, and the boat slowed as if on a leash before nosing gently up to a granite monolith surrounded by hardstem bulrush.

My hunting partner, Dave Kay, and I jumped out, secured the line and set about unloading our gear. With shotguns, shells and seats safely stashed, we began tossing decoys from the shoreline blind, while Stephen used the boat to strategically deploy the rest of the blocks downwind of our hiding place. Once we'd all shared a thumbs-up in acknowledgement of agreement on the pattern of decoys, Stephen waved a quick goodbye and once again the outboard roared to life. Within seconds, he'd disappeared around the point, and Dave and I settled in with the anticipation that only waterfowlers can know.

We didn't have long to wait. As if synchronized with the sun's struggle to push its way over the distant horizon, the first flight of birds whispered through the blocks just as the earliest warming splinters of morning light danced around our blind. Although experiences as spectacular as those that greeted us daily on Lake of the Woods can never be described as routine, Dave and I paused only briefly between flights to share smiles that clearly affirmed, "Here we go again!"

༄

Prior to this trip, my experiences on Lake of the Woods were limited to a handful of summer evenings fishing walleye and smallmouth bass on Whitefish Bay in the easternmost region of the vast lake. Those brief tastes had been enough; however, to convince me that this was a place I had to get to know more intimately. So, when Randy and Maureen Hanson of historic Hanson's Wilderness Lodges offered to host Dave Kay and me for five days in October, I didn't hesitate for any longer than it took to "x" out the days on my calendar. Beyond the fishing that has earned Lake of the Woods an international reputation, we would also have the opportunity to experience a full suite of the area's hunting, including waterfowl, upland birds and white-tailed deer, the full "cast and blast" agenda!

Our first day in camp began as most do, with time spent unpacking, getting to know lodge procedures and generally settling in, all the while trying hard not to let your smile betray the impatience to get in the field that lurks, barely restrained, right below the surface. Randy Hanson, lodge owner/operator all his life, clearly understood our angst and soon had us aboard a Cessna 185 on floats for a brief reconnaissance to Ajax Lake. Ajax serves as one of Hanson's Lodges outpost camps, hosting fishermen in the summer and moose hunters each fall. We went in with Stephen, Randy's son and the third generation of Hanson lodge owner/operators, to ensure that the outpost was ready to be closed up for the winter. The flight allowed us an unparalleled perspective of the broader Lake of the Woods region and confirmed for us just how much true wilderness remains in the region. While unmistakable signs of the logging industry are evident through parts of the area, much of it appears to have seen little human disturbance. A verdant landscape pockmarked with endless ponds and lakes, it's easy to understand how excited 20-year-old Jacques De Noyon must have been when he became the first white man to see Lake of the Woods and surroundings in 1688. As a scout and explorer pushing west in search of new land to trap, he quickly recognized the natural productivity of the area, naming the immense new water body "Lake of the Isles."

As we cruised toward Ajax, it quickly became clear why the outpost is so popular with moose hunters. We spotted more than a dozen moose on the short flight in, including a few good bulls, and undoubtedly flew over many more that were hidden under the dense canopy of trees below. Our time at Ajax was brief, just long enough for Stephen to ensure the camp was ready for winter, then we were back in the air and headed for King Island in the heart of Sabaskong Bay on the eastern edge of Lake of the Woods.

King Island, while only seven acres, has been home to thousands of adventure-seeking anglers over the years. Established 80 years ago, by Kendall Hanson in 1926, the island is home to the Hanson's most renowned facility, King Island Lodge, a small assortment of beautiful and classic cabins nestled in a grove of towering white pines. The main lodge and five of the nine guest cabins were built before 1930, though all feature the full suite of conveniences expected in a modern full-service lodge. Wandering through and among the buildings, the aura of tradition and nostalgia was unmistakable.

Evidence of the island's great heritage was everywhere: a beautiful hand-built birch bark canoe hung suspended over the bar; wooden decoys, including several classic Mason blocks, sat perched on shelves and mantles, proudly displaying scars won through years of honest use; handfuls of antique fishing lures collecting dust beneath aged photos of gentlemen in fedoras hoisting huge fish aloft. Hanging under the eaves of one small cabin, I even noticed the gaping, open-mouthed mounted head of a huge muskie. It had been years since I'd seen one of these once-popular trophies, but it was clearly at home on this historic island. Although I would have loved to have spent the night at the lodge and further experienced her charms, Randy wanted to nose around a nearby bay where deer had been seen regularly, and neither Dave nor I had to be told twice when it was time to transport our gear from the airplane and into the boat that would take us to our hunting spot.

While that evening didn't produce a buck for either of us, the does we did see and the fresh sign that saturated the area left little doubt plenty of deer made their homes in these woods. And, while still-hunting my way through the unfamiliar area, I stumbled across a hidden lake that held more than 1000 ring-necked ducks, clear evidence that the waterfowl, too, were holding in good numbers locally.

The difficulty with all buffets of course, is being careful not to fill up on the first couple of offerings and finding yourself unable to take advantage of those items that appear farther down the line. Dave and I both recognized that we would have to be careful not to overindulge in one or two activities if we were going to enjoy all the area had to offer. So, that evening back at the lodge, we worked out a rough schedule with Randy. The next day we focus on fishing, with black crappie at the top of our wish list.

Our insistence that we focus on crappies caught Randy by surprise. Those seeking fame, trophies or glamour tend to focus on the lake's more notorious fish. Famous walleye anglers, renowned muskie hunters and well-known bass fisherman regularly ply Lake of the Woods in search of the outsized trophies she's been known to give up. As far as I know, there are no famous crappie fishermen. If there were, however, no doubt they'd spend time here as well because the lake has no shortage of them. Dave and I have both enjoyed the opportunity to angle for many of the more popular fish species on this and other quality lakes over the years, but neither of us had ever caught a "mess 'o crappies" before, and we were bound and determined to try on this trip. Besides being notoriously difficult to target throughout the year, and somewhat finicky even when located, crappie also enjoy the reputation for being the best "table fish" that swims, at least according to many whose opinions carry some weight. We simply had to find out for ourselves.

We were joined in the morning by Gerald Arch, a local Indigenous man who grew up on and around the lake, and provided occasional guiding services for the Hanson family. With Stephen and I in one boat, and Gerald and Dave in another, we made the long run to a favourite crappie hole. It turned up empty, as did the next couple. *True to form*, I thought, remembering what many have told me about trying to find crappie when you want them. With Gerald fixated on his electronics, he directed us out a little deeper in the next promising location. It was Dave who connected first, hooking up with a beautiful, dark crappie at the 12-metre depth.

Crappie are not big fish, with a two-pounder considered a real dandy, but when you're taking them on light line down deep as we were, they can be a real challenge to hook and put up a surprisingly enthusiastic tussle.

Our technique was simple as we bounced ¼-ounce jigs tipped with minnows a foot or so off the bottom. Crappie, or at least these, take the bait lightly, and we lost considerably more bait than we landed crappie. But it was a beautiful, warm midday, and every few minutes one of us would hoist up a real slab of a fish; intense black splotches contrasting spectacularly against a background hue of yellow-green. By the time we decided to pull anchor, we'd landed nearly three dozen of the scrappy panfish, keeping enough of the better ones to ensure a great feed later in the week. It was difficult at the time to imagine that the day could get any more exciting, but it would prove to do just that.

We drifted under the bright midday sun, contentedly eating our lunches and discussing our options for the afternoon. Loons trilled in the background, bald eagles soared overhead and we saw no other boats. The traffic on Lake of the Woods peters out to a trickle shortly after the Labour Day weekend, and at times it appeared we had the enormous lake to ourselves. Gerald knew of some islands that often hold bucks escaping the pressure of shore-bound hunters, and as Dave and I had packed our hunting gear along with our tackle, we decided to make the half-hour run to the area he was suggesting.

Islands have long been favoured habitats for deer hunters. A hunter or two are posted at one end while the others "push" through the thickest cover in hopes that an unsuspecting deer will walk past a posted hunter in its efforts to stay ahead of the pushers. More often than not, mature bucks will find a way to circle back behind the pushers or, demonstrating nerves of steel garnered through years of experience, hold tight as pushers stroll by within mere metres. Either way, the result of most island pushes is little more than a brisk though enjoyable afternoon walk. Such was the case with the first two islands we pushed. Dave and I alternated in the roles of poster and pusher, and though unfruitful as far as whitetails went, the exercise was an appreciated respite after several hours in the boat.

The last island was the largest of the three, so Stephen and Gerald decided that the best strategy was to go with both Dave and I on post, while the two of them did their best to zigzag through the dense understory. Stephen dropped us off at one end of the island before boating back to join Gerald for the coordinated push. Dave and I had some time to locate and identify the best potential ambush sites, with Dave electing to post at the first of the two.

As we coordinated our plan, I checked my gear before pressing on. Ontario's law is that all big game hunters must where blaze orange, and I readjusted the Velcro closure on the cheap vest I was wearing over my hunting jacket. As Dave mumbled something about me looking like I was wearing "a blaze-orange sports bra," I strutted away cross island with as much pride as I could muster under the circumstances, parking myself a hundred yards or so from his chosen vantage. All the while, I contemplated an appropriate retort to spring on him at the next available opportunity.

I settled in among the rocks of a natural protuberance, leaning back against one particularly smooth boulder. Out of the wind, and with the early afternoon sun warming me,

I think I was half asleep when the sound of Dave's shot brought me to full alert. He was too far away to holler to for explanation, so I quickly decided that my safest and most practical option was to stay put for the time being. It couldn't have been more than a minute later that I heard someone, or something, crashing through the underbrush, heading right toward me. I strained to identify the intruder through the thick cover, and was soon able to discern the unmistakable shape of an antler before it disappeared from view. I raised my rifle to the ready position, and when the buck emerged from cover a mere 25 metres or so away, and closing, I held on the point of his shoulder and squeezed.

As it turned out I needn't have taken the shot because it was the same buck Dave had shot at moments before, with his bullet passing perfectly through both lungs. Later, upon examining the blood trail, it was clear the buck wouldn't have gone much farther, but my bullet had done little meat damage and at least we didn't have to search through the nearly impenetrable cover for a downed animal. Dave had also been relaxing in the warmth of the sun when the buck came trotting down the trail, exactly according to the plan.

Although the animal wasn't one of the huge old bucks that northwest Ontario enjoys a growing reputation for producing—several examples of which were mounted in the main lodge at the Hanson's camp—it was a mature buck in rut and a fine whitetail by any standards. In short order, we took photos, cleaned the deer and loaded it into the boat. A quick look at our watches told us that several hours remained of the day. We could head back to camp now, or we could…

Rummaging through all the gear in the boats, Dave and I emerged with our shotguns and the kind of grins typically reserved for little boys hoping their mischievous inclinations will be overlooked in favour of their blatant attempt to appear cute. Stephen and Gerald had reported earlier that they'd located a hidden bay chockfull of ring-necked ducks, and the opportunity to get in among them was more than Dave or I could even consider postponing.

Diving duck hunting is a true passion that Dave and I share, and we make it a point to spend a few days together in this pursuit each fall. However, while I lean more towards bluebills as my favourite, Dave is an unabashed nut for ring-necks or "blackjacks" as some call them colloquially. The seeds of this passion were sewn in him as a youth while hunting divers in southern Ontario but really blossomed during the 10 years or so he spent as a waterfowl biologist in the Northwest Territories. Twice over the years I've had the opportunity to hunt with him in the north for these hefty little bundles of feathered wildness, and I have come to clearly understand how they have eloped with his hunter's heart. And while I was certainly keen to give the hidden bay a try, Dave was absolutely beside himself with enthusiasm.

The run in the boat from our deer island to where we'd be hunting ducks was a good hour, and I leaned back quietly in my chair, unable in any case to easily talk over the outboard's hum. Not that I felt much like conversation at that point; I was too busy reflecting on all I'd experienced in the few short days since arriving at Lake of the Woods.

I'm at an age where I think occasionally about retirement, or more to the point, about where I might like to settle down once I do retire. As an avid outdoorsman, my thoughts revolve most often around the places that will allow me to enjoy the greatest number of the activities I love. As we skipped across the great lake, with nothing but blue water, blue skies and green forests for as far as the eye could see, I couldn't help but think it would be difficult to find a more perfect sportsman's paradise than Lake of the Woods. World-class fishing, big game and bird game hunting all in one spot. At the very least, this was clearly emerging as an area that would warrant further investigation and consideration in the years ahead.

The duck hunt that evening was everything we could have imagined and more. Hundreds upon hundreds upon hundreds of ringnecks piled into the bay, often in swarming tornados of birds. Dave and I sat on a granite promontory at the entrance to the bay, 10 metres or so above the water's surface. A little brush piled in front of us broke up our silhouette, and an aged white pine loomed above us, ensuring we'd not be betrayed from above. The birds arrived in waves for nearly an hour, with seldom more than a few minutes between flights. After the first couple of flurries, Dave and I leaned back and simply watched the natural spectacle that was unfolding before us. We had neither the inclination nor the need to take a limit of birds that evening; somehow focusing on a bag limit would have diminished, rather than enhanced, the hunt. We could see Gerald and Stephen gesturing quizzically from where they were hidden farther down the shoreline, clearly not understanding why these two hunters who had travelled so far to get to this opportunity were now opting not to shoot on what was arguably as fine a duck hunt as anyone could hope to experience. We would explain it later to them as best we could, somewhat apologetically in respect for their efforts in making it all happen, but it was difficult to articulate. We had responded to something we felt rather than something we thought, and attempting to describe or interpret those feelings left us both somewhat at a loss for words.

As we recalled our day from the comfort of our cabin that night, Dave and I couldn't help but comment on our "boreal trifecta." Black crappies, white-tailed deer and ring-necked ducks; it's difficult to imagine a trio of creatures more perfectly representing the wilderness of northern Ontario than those three. "Game to the core" as Dave likes to describe wild creatures native to Canada's rugged Shield. Before the week was out, we would experience even more of what Lake of the Woods has to offer. Canvasbacks, wood ducks, mallards, wigeon, scaup, goldeneye and buffleheads would all take their turns over our blocks. At midday we'd bring out the rods, jigging or trolling up smallmouth bass, walleye, perch and pike. And on one sunny afternoon, we beached on an island and took our shotguns for a walk down an old abandoned trail, ending back at the water's edge an hour later with four fat ruffed grouse in hand.

Eventually, it was time to head home, and as we drove up the highway towards Winnipeg and our flight back to Alberta, I couldn't help but wonder how I'd overlooked this magnificent resource for so many years. Perhaps contemporary philosopher Susanne Langer was right when she suggested, "Most new discoveries are suddenly seen things that were always there."

13

BIRDS OF A DIFFERENT FEATHER

I got to know Len Everett when I was an employee of Ducks Unlimited Canada, where he served on the conservation company's Board of Directors. If you strip away all the fancy talk, he was, quite simply, a nice man who always had time for whoever wanted his attention. Turn the page a few years and I started to get an itch to hunt sea ducks. As an avid water-fowler, it was one of the few Canadian duck hunts I'd yet to experience. There are no established sea duck guiding services on Vancouver Island, so I figured who better to call than Len to ask if he had a few days to show me around the awe-inspiring landscape and seascape where he's lived all his life and introduce me to the thrill that is sea duck hunting. Always the gentleman, Len readily agreed. It's a debt I'll never be able to repay.

It's January 2, and I'm sitting on a gravel spit off Tree Island, north of Denman Island and near the entrance to Vancouver Island's Comox Harbour. Overhead, the familiar yellow of a Canadian Armed Forces search-and-rescue aircraft circles the harbour in an apparent training exercise, a stark reminder that mistakes in this environment can cost you everything in mere moments.

The temperature's hovering right around freezing, there's a moderate breeze and the choppy ocean swells are releasing a mist that covers everything, including me. This is cold-to-the-bone hunting, but I'm prepared for it, wearing several layers; neoprene waders; waterproof gloves; and a warm, water-repellent hat. Fortunately, there's little cloud cover, and the sun is warming my face as I sit in anticipation, waiting for the first flight of sea ducks to swing over the blocks.

The tide was at its highest at first light, and it's been receding throughout the day, slowly exposing new ground from beneath the swells. I check my watch. It's 2:30 PM, and in 12 hours, the spit I'm sitting on will have once again disappeared beneath the waves.

From my vantage point, I can make out several species of sea ducks bobbing on the dark waters of the harbour. Surf, black and white-winged scoters are here, as are clown-coloured harlequins and striking long-tailed ducks. One minute they're riding a swell, the next they're gone. It appears they're feeding, as periodically I see them diving. Few are flying. What I do see on the wing are mallards, bufflehead and common goldeneyes, but I'm not here for those species that I can hunt back home in Alberta. As I look north, I can also make out the unmistakeable profile of skeins of brant trading across the open water in the distance, but there's no open season for those iconic birds here.

Patience is paramount for waterfowlers in any environment, but perhaps never more so than when hunting sea ducks. And patience is easy in this wondrous seascape. Behind me on the mainland, snow-capped mountains gird the urban development along the shore, while out front, forested islands stand sentinel as gatekeepers to the mysteries of the Strait of Georgia. For a prairie boy like me, the view never gets old.

Eventually, my perseverance pays off, and a small flight of white-winged scoters skirts the outer edge of the short line of decoys. I rise and swing, focused on the drake at the head of the line. At the report, I see a bird tumble into the water, but it's not the drake I'd targeted. It's a hen that goes down, two birds behind the drake in the string of five, a vivid reminder that large-bodied sea ducks are often farther away and flying more quickly than they appear. And the open salt chuck offers little in the way of benchmarks for gauging distance and speed.

Thirty metres farther up the spit, my host, Len Everett, rises from where he'd been reclining against a log. "We'd better get the boat." he says matter-of-factly. "That scoter isn't dead, and they can cover a lot of water when wounded."

We quickly clamber into Len's Boston Whaler, push off the beach and motor toward where we last saw the bird dive. This is no place for a retriever; the cold water and extended distances make for a lethal combination. I scan the grey waters and spot a blob floating in the swells 100 metres ahead, so I point Len in its direction. By the time we get there, the bird is floating lifeless. I use a long-handled fishing net to scoop it into the boat. My first-ever sea duck.

I manage to drop a second white-winged scoter later on that first afternoon of our two-day hunt, and fortunately, it falls stone dead. I then find a way to gas shots on successive pairs of long-tailed ducks that cruised the outer reaches of our blocks. It's not an auspicious sea duck–hunting debut by any measure, but Len had given me fair warning that day one is typically a humbling experience for first-timers.

On day two, Len and I headed out with a renewed optimism that was almost immediately rewarded. Shortly after first light, we motored to the middle of the harbour, shut down the engine and let the boat drift with the current. Behind us, a dozen decoys on a longline obediently followed. There, out on the open water, our quarry was long-tailed ducks and harlequins.

The long-tails were highly visible, sprinkled like grains of salt on the grey water of the harbour, but the colourful harlies appeared to be scarce. Surprisingly, few harlequins are seen in the harbour these days, Len says, adding that he's concerned nobody seems to care or ask why. Perhaps they've simply moved to more productive waters, or they may truly be on the decline. In the greater Comox Valley area, where Len has hunted most of his life, he believes the numbers of sea ducks overall are down over the long term with no appreciable recent increases.

Long-tailed ducks seldom venture near the islands or mainland, preferring the safety of open water, but at least one flight, distracted by our decoys, showed little concern for our boat. As they cut through our line I rose and swung ahead of the first bird, a beautiful full-plumage drake. I watched it splash down out of the corner of my eye as I searched for a second target.

Banking hard, two more drakes turned downwind to escape. I pushed the barrel out in front of the lead bird, squeezed the trigger and it also splashed down at the report. We collected both ducks in short order. It was the first time I'd ever held these spectacular birds in my hands. I was somewhat surprised by how small-bodied they were—almost dainty given the vast, brutish habitat they prefer.

After that first successful volley, the action quieted down significantly. In response, we moved around the harbour, setting up in several different locations on the open water and on a series of small islands. With little wind to encourage them, however, the birds just weren't moving.

Early in the afternoon Len beached us on an island where he's historically had success. The island was relatively long and serpentine, having cobbled and sandy shores littered with driftwood of all shapes and sizes. On the highest points that remained above water at high tide, withered grasses and a few wind-buffeted trees eked out a meagre existence. And here and there, watchful bald eagles perched on the driftwood.

We strung out two-dozen scoter blocks and a sprinkling of goldeneyes in the open water about 25 metres offshore then leaned back against a beached log. We were hoping the birds would become more active, and we didn't have to wait long. A flight of surf scoters arrived first, and I pulled a stunning drake from the mix. In breeding plumage, these are hefty, striking ducks with velvet-black bodies contrasted against a nape and forehead of snow white. They have oversized rosy-pink webbed feet and a broad bill with its beautiful palette of yellow, orange, white and black. From afar they may look uniformly dull and dark, but in the hand they're as brilliantly coloured as any duck I've seen.

Graciously, Len pushed off to retrieve my downed surf scoter before it could drift too far, leaving me to continue my vigil from shore. And just about the time he slowed down to scoop up the bird, another small skein of white-winged scoters rounded the bend of an adjacent island clearly hell-bent for the decoys. As I rose and swung my gun to get out in front of them, the birds turned and gained speed, making for the safety of open water. By then I was becoming more accustomed to judging the speed and distance of these ducks; I shot twice with more confidence than I ought to have, dropping two birds in quick succession. My timing was perfect, and Len was able to pick them up on his way back.

Over the next few hours, flock after flock of scoters—surf and white-winged—cruised through to examine our decoys. But with several birds in hand, I didn't want to shoot another scoter unless it was an elusive black; I still hadn't taken a harlequin and didn't want to risk limiting out before I had that opportunity.

With time on our hands, Len spoke of growing up in the Comox Valley, where he'd hunted and fished all his life. He once even guided John Wayne, "the Duke" himself, for salmon. But times have changed in the valley. While recreational fishing remains popular, Len says the culture of sea duck hunting has all but disappeared. That was clearly in evidence, since that day we were the only hunters on the water.

With only an hour to go until sundown, we decided to pack up and move once again. We motored back out to open water and dropped our decoy rig, once again adrift on the swells. It would be our last chance to find harlies. Failing that, perhaps we could fool more long-tailed ducks.

Sure enough, we hadn't been in place long before a squadron of a half-dozen long-tails broke from their flight path and veered toward our decoys. It was decision time. If I took a couple of those birds I'd be limited out, meaning I'd go home without a harlequin. On the other hand, if I didn't shoot, I could easily be squandering the final opportunity of our hunt.

In the end, it was an easy decision. I hadn't come here to shoot bag limits, rather to experience everything that West Coast sea duck hunting has to offer. So, I let the long-tails swing unmolested through the blocks, content to take a pass on the easiest shots of the day.

Hunting can be fickle. Sometimes you're treated like a prince; at other times like a pauper, worthy of little more than disdain. There's simply no predicting which way it will go on any given day. But on that afternoon, hunting the most majestic of all waterfowl on the dark waters of Comox Harbour, I felt as I was treated like royalty.

Not two minutes after I passed on the long-tails, three harlequins—two drakes and a hen—appeared out of nowhere, their dark blue plumage nearly invisible as they winged toward us just a metre or so above the swells.

Len's trained eyes spotted them first, and at his alert, I reacted on instinct. Quickly picking out the drakes, I shot twice. Only one splashed down; however, and the remaining drake and hen wheeled safely away, quickly disappearing against the backdrop of the harbour. Just as well, I figured, knowing the pair would help ensure a new generation of sea ducks would continue to trade across the grey, misty skies of Comox Harbour.

14

UNGAVA ADVENTURE DIARY

Sometimes it's the place you remember most. Occasionally it's the fish you caught or the game you shot. But when I think of this visit to Québec's Ungava region, it's the people that resonate most strongly. Specifically young Luke Sorrell and his father, who were in camp to help Luke live out his dream of hunting caribou, and Sammy Cantafio and his team, who were determined that Luke's aspiration would come true. It was with great sadness that I was notified less than a year after this hunt of Luke's passing, succumbing to the many ailments he'd been battling all his life. I take solace in remembering our time together and grateful that I was there to see his dream realized.

It's been said that a promise made is a debt unpaid, and the weight of this particular IOU abated only as we lifted from the tarmac in Kuujjuaq, two air hours north of Montréal. The skies were clear, and save for mechanical failures, there'd be no turning back. The Air Inuit Twin Otter clawed its way into the western sky, destination Gordon Lake and the heart of the Ungava region's annual caribou migration. It had been 10 years since I'd last visited Kuujjuaq, formerly known as Fort Chimo, the typical jumping off point for those who fish and hunt in Québec's most northern region. On that fateful previous trip, I'd spent six frustrating days in town as a howling early blizzard grounded all small aircraft, keeping me and many other anxious hunters from getting out to remote caribou camps. Eventually, I'd simply turned south again and gone home, but with a promise that one day I'd return and experience firsthand the angling and hunting opportunities that abound across Ungava's rugged landscapes.

When I was finally granted the opportunity to return to Ungava, with Sammy Cantafio's renowned Ungava Adventures no less (regarded by many as the premiere outfitter in northern Québec), I didn't hesitate for a second. A little juggling of my schedule to make the trip a reality was an insignificant burden, and as Kuujjuaq disappeared behind us along with the tree line, I relaxed in the comfort that this time I wouldn't have to head home early.

The flight to camp was a quick hour and fifteen minutes, and I spent the entire time with my face pressed to the glass, watching as the transition from boreal forest to tundra unfolded below me—a landscape dominated by spruce giving way to the open, pockmarked features of the northern ecozone. Eventually, the coniferous trees were only able to carve out a meager existence along the edges of lakeshores and in low-lying areas.

The first impression as you fly over the tundra leads you to believe that the landscape below is flat and featureless, save for the sprinkling of lakes and ponds, but on closer inspection you realize how deceptive that perspective is. The landscape is anything but flat, with numerous escarpments, ridges and rolling hills dominating. The retreat of the last glaciers some 10,000 years earlier is also clearly evident in the striations etched on the broad face of the granite outcroppings, the sinewy eskers that snake across the terrain and the moraines of accumulated sand, gravel and rock. As we neared our destination, I could see increasing numbers of caribou below, a living testament to the true vitality of this apparently barren environment.

The Twin Otter touched down after a quick descent, landing atop an esker on the shore of Lake Gordon. From the time the wheels first touched to the point at which we stopped rolling, the plane couldn't have covered more than 100 metres; the versatility and capability of these Canadian-built workhorse aircraft never ceases to amaze me. As the camp staff met the plane and began the task of unloading, I got a chance to meet the other hunters with whom I'd be sharing camp. There were five of us in total because this was opening week in camp, and Sammy prefers a small group of hunters while the staff work out the kinks and gain understanding of how and where the caribou migration is unfolding. My hunting companions were Neil and Susan Armstrong, a husband and wife from Rochester, N.Y., and Mitch and Luke Sorrell, a father and his 12-year-old son from

Indiana. Also on the trip was Gene Bidlespacher, a renowned videographer who would be filming our experience as part of a three-week stint he was working for Ungava Adventures.

As the aircraft departed in a cloud of dust and gravel from atop the narrow esker, we made our way along the 200-metre path to camp, which was a cluster of small plywood buildings perched on the edge of the lake. We were assigned our respective cabins, and I was pleased to be bunking with Mitch and Luke. We quickly chose bunks, unpacked then gathered in the camp kitchen for a hot lunch, a chance to meet the staff and the opportunity to learn what the daily agenda would be.

The Gordon Lake camp staff consisted of manager Fabian Kennedy and his wife Peggy, who handled all the kitchen duties. We also met Bucky Adams, Sammy's lead guide and right-hand man. Bucky would be making the hunting decisions, and his easy confidence helped settle the first-day jitters all hunters experience in a new camp.

Within two hours of landing, we were out on the tundra and anxious to explore our new surroundings and get face-to-face with the caribou that brought us here. We were hunting Québec's infamous Leaf River herd, a massive gathering of caribou that migrate almost continually throughout the year in an ovate pattern to the west and southwest of Ungava Bay. Calving takes place annually at the northern apex of the route, with Gordon Lake strategically situated along the path that takes them to their southern wintering grounds. To the east of us a mere handful of miles, the George River herd was replicating a yearly sojourn, following their own time-tested migratory circuit. Although both herds offer spectacular hunting opportunities, the Leaf River herd is generally regarded as supporting bulls with larger, fuller racks. Unlike the clustered migration associated with herds of other species, such as Africa's famed wildebeest, caribou are more scattered in their migratory movements. The herd itself is a loose conglomeration of animals, incorporating thousands of small clusters of animals, and the migration can stretch in excess of 150 kilometres in every direction at any one time. The rutted trails imbedded in the tundra offer clear evidence that a pattern exists amid the apparent chaos.

As Bucky took Mitch and Luke off in one direction, and Sue and Neil headed off in another, I ambled parallel to the lakeshore, northward, in the direction from which caribou were arriving. As I walked I could see small groups of animals flowing across the landscape in that ground-eating manner of walking that only caribou display. Like Mario Lemieux in his prime, caribou may appear slow, but if they get past you, you'll never catch up to them. I've learned from previous hunts that the best strategy is to select a vantage point from which to watch as they appear on the horizon, glassing for outstanding bulls. If you see one worth investigating, the trick is to anticipate where he's headed and hustle to a potential interception point. Guess wrong, and you're left with no option than to focus back on the horizon and start glassing anew.

I made my way to a likely lookout point on the crest of a natural rise, hiding behind an eight-foot high boulder that stood as a lone sentry on the hill's crest. It wasn't long before I saw caribou picking their way over the hill on the horizon about three kilometres distant. I was in no hurry to shoot an animal unless it was an especially impressive specimen, and over the next few hours, I laid against my rock in the afternoon sun and watched as nearly 200 caribou passed within easy shooting range. Particularly intriguing, beyond the impressive racks of the mature bulls, were the many caribou calves, furry little bundles of dirty white down sporting coal-black noses and eyes. No puppy has anything on these little creatures in the cuteness department. Five separate caribou walked within 20 metres of my hiding spot, including one fairly impressive bull that sauntered past at less than five metres, completely unaware of my presence until the snap of my camera shutter shocked him into a trot, his loose ankle bones clicking against the uneven terrain. Eventually, I headed back to camp, content in the knowledge that if the next few days revealed as many caribou as the first afternoon did, I'd enjoy lots of opportunity to find a good bull.

Over supper that night, we exchanged tales of our afternoon hunts. Mitch had been the only successful hunter, taking a nice bull with his bow. It was difficult to be sure given the sheer number of caribou in the area, but it looked identical to the bull that had strolled by my monolith on the hill earlier that afternoon. With a 5:45 AM wake-up call on the menu, we headed to our bunks at 10:30. Before turning in, I stole a final glimpse at the red orb of Mars as it sat above the lakeshore on its closest visit to Earth in more than 1000 years.

On day two, I headed out with Bucky, Luke, Mitch and Gene, the four of us riding on a little trailer as Bucky towed us behind a quad to the far end of the esker. From there we set off on foot, glassing as we went. There was no shortage of caribou, and by my estimation we saw in excess of 3000 animals before nightfall. Our primary goal that morning was to find a bull for young Luke, and I was more than

happy to take a back seat in the priority line to this courageous young boy.

Luke and his Dad had been awarded this hunting trip
through the combined generosity of the Hunt Of A Lifetime
organization and Sammy Cantafio. Luke suffered numerous
health issues all of his young life. He was only 23 days old
when he received a heart transplant, and his life since had
been plagued with a variety of ailments, ranging from kidney
disease to a paralyzed diaphragm that left him with the effective use of only one lung. Pneumonia was an almost annual
occurrence for Luke, and his daily regimen included a seemingly endless stream of pills and a carefully monitored diet.
Difficulties such as these would render most of us mired in
self-pity, but not Luke. As I learned more from his dad of the
daily hurdles Luke faced, my admiration for him grew in
exponential leaps. Far from feeling sorry for his plight, Luke
quickly established himself as the enthusiastic leader of our
hunting camp, using his keen mind and sharp wit to trade
good-natured ribbing with everyone as is often the nature of
friendly hunting camps. As the days unfolded, I became
attached to Luke as did all in camp, and as the years go by, it
is his inspirational courage that I recall first from this hunt.

Hunting luck was with us that morning, and under
Bucky's guidance, Luke got situated behind a large rock just
before a small herd of caribou crested a small rise some
75 metres away. At Bucky's nod and Luke's affirmation that
he was ready, a single shot from his 7mm–08 broke the
silence, and an impressive bull went down. I don't suspect
any of our group was far from shedding a tear of joy as we
shared in Luke's obvious elation with his trophy. His initial
success was short-lived; however, because not 15 minutes

later, before we'd even completed the obligatory back slap-
ping and hand shaking that accompanies such an occasion,
another group of caribou, including an even larger bull, came
ambling along the same path.

We all scrambled to hide, and at Bucky's inquiry, Luke
nodded a quick assent; he was more than ready and willing to
fill his second tag on the full-antlered bull that was closing in
by the second. As Bucky got Luke resettled and reloaded,
a sudden thought occurred to him, and he looked my way
with a clear though unspoken question. It's an age-old tenet
that in any hunting camp, when practical, all hunters have an
opportunity to take a first animal before others shoot their
second. Given the circumstance, I was amazed that Bucky
had recognized this and looked to me for support. He needn't
have, of course. I was more than happy to let Luke take
advantage of the situation at hand, but it told me a lot about
the type of guide and person that Bucky was. I was grateful
that he'd thought to consider the issue in that light at all.

At the crack of the single shot, a second bull went
down. Luke was delighted, and I don't suppose you could
have wiped the smiles off the rest of us if you'd tried, especially the ear-to-ear grin on the face of his justifiably proud
father.

Later, in what was becoming an increasingly wet and
windy day, I took my first bull, a wide-racked male that we'd
watched since it first crossed a hill into view a mile and a half
away. He was travelling with two other mature bulls; we'd
guessed correctly about where they would cross a small lake
and were lying in wait when they did. With three nice caribou
racks and some prime table fare in tow, it was a pretty upbeat
crew that arrived back in camp that evening. We were even

more tickled to learn upon arrival that Susan had also scored on her first bull, taking it with a 20-gauge slug no less.

The next day dawned less favourably. The relatively nice weather we'd enjoyed the previous day was getting progressively worse, and a cold wind and horizontal rain greeted us as we stretched from our slumber. Mitch took his second bull at first light, making a fine 170-yard shot. With both of them now tagged out, and given the deteriorating conditions, it was only natural that Mitch take Luke back to camp rather than stay out in the nasty stuff. The caribou were less active that day, though I suspect it was mere coincidence because conditions we find uncomfortable barely register with animals so uniquely adapted to the climate.

While Gene set up on a traditional caribou crossing point hoping for some close-up footage, Bucky and I ventured farther away from camp to one of the high ridges that girded the area we'd been hunting. As I got to know Bucky better, it was easy to discern how and why he'd become a leader for Sammy's outfitting business. The quintessential guide in nearly every respect, Bucky is tall and slim, with the broad shoulders and narrow hips of one who's accustomed to hard work. He smiles easily, is clearly well educated, and with his litany of entertaining stories of the many caribou and bear hunts he's guided always within easy grasp, Bucky has that enviable way of making all those around him feel at ease and comfortable.

The highlight of our day came early in the afternoon when Bucky and I were able to locate and then sneak to within spitting distance of a family group of musk ox known to frequent the area. Remnants of a translocation of musk oxen into the Ungava region years earlier, the group consisted of a bull, a mature cow, a sub-adult and a calf. Although uneasy with our presence at first, they quickly accepted that we were no threat and tolerated us for 20 minutes before ambling off, undoubtedly in search of more privacy. Having never before seen musk ox at such close quarters, I was thoroughly trans-fixed by the encounter.

The following day's hunt was my last because Bucky, Gene and I were scheduled to fly out the following morning to another lake where we'd spend a few days fishing for brookies and lake trout. The weather was a little better as the five of us struck out, but I felt no pressure to take a second animal. I'd not arrived with the mindset that I needed to shoot two caribou, and with a good bull hanging in camp, I was already more than satisfied. Besides, I'd had literally hundreds of opportunities to fill a second tag if I'd been in a hurry to do so. Nevertheless, when a group of eight bulls started showing signs of nearing our vantage point atop an esker some five kilometres from camp, my interest piqued when one appeared to be among the largest of the thousands of caribou I'd assessed since arriving.

Picking out a trophy caribou bull is always a challenge. To those of us more accustomed to evaluating deer, moose or elk, all caribou look impressive with their over-sized racks perched on top of relatively small bodies. Telling the good ones from the not-so-good is an endless trade-off of attri-butes; one must assess their top points, bottom points, bez and shovels, while also estimating their overall height and width. Despite these complexities, when you see a really good one you know it immediately, and one bull among the group headed our way was clearly a dandy. He was 150 metres below and walking parallel to us when I touched off the .25-06, and in that moment, my caribou hunt was over.

Gene, Bucky and I climbed aboard a Beaver on floats the next morning, tipping our wings as we flew across Gordon Lake in a gesture of congratulations to Sue, who was just finishing up caping her second caribou after a long stalk at first light across the lake from camp. After a half-hour flight, we dropped into Lake Sabrina, boated across in an aluminum car topper, then hiked a half-mile down to the churning waters of the Lefebvre River. I've long believed that brook trout are the prettiest fish that swim, and it had been an aspiration of mine for years to fish for them in the cold, clean waters where they are native. So to be in a region where honest-to-goodness five-, six- and even seven-pounders swim had me flush with anticipation.

The Lefebvre was everything a brook trout river should be—transparent waters tumbling over rock ledges with reckless abandon, creating a patchwork of pools, eddies, runs and tails, all prime trout-holding water. I tied a Muddler Minnow pattern to my eight-weight floating line, but it quickly became apparent that in the turbulent water the buoyant fly floated too high in the water column. Searching through my fly box, I settled on a bead-head Bow River Bugger, a pattern created for the rainbows and browns that ply the waters of Alberta's renowned Bow River. Casting the fly down and across the tailout of a pool, I soon had my first take. After a short but vigorous tussle, I held the trout aloft, more for my own admiration than for the benefit of the others. The fish was as stunning as those I'd seen in magazine photos over the years, stout and broad-backed with colourful halos bespeckling a deep olive-green back, which in turn gave way to a crimson belly. From the belly emerged the species' tell-tale fins with their shocking white leading edges contrasting sharply against a thin black border. I estimated its weight at two-and-a-half pounds, snapped a few quick photos then released it gingerly back to its ice-water home.

Over the next hour and a half, I landed several more equally stunning brookies, the best topping 20 inches and tipping the scales at about three-and-a-half pounds. This was the realization of what had compelled me to return to Ungava, catching native brook trout in their natural waters, an all too quickly disappearing opportunity. As I released my last fish of the day, it struck me that the one thing I'd not anticipated was how gingerly these fish were taking my flies. I'd expected that wild brook trout would be tackle-smashing brutes, punishing any and all creatures that dared set foot or fin into waters over which they were clearly lord and master. Instead, these trout behaved more like perfect little ladies and gentlemen, almost apologetic in the way they took my offerings. Their refined behaviour, however, turned downright rude once they recognized they'd been duped, and in the family tradition of all char, put up a fight as though their very lives depended upon it (which I'm sure in their minds it did).

We left the Lefebvre in time to fly to Sammy's camp at nearby Napier Lake where we settled in for the night. We were up early the next morning to fish, but the North's infamous nemesis, the weather, was clearly plotting against us. Despite our second thoughts, however, we braved the growing wind and teeming rain. Unfortunately the fish, too, seemed to have better days on their mind, and by most accounts refused to cooperate. Bucky did manage to hook and land a 20-pound lake trout, but with few exceptions the brookies turned up their delicate noses at nearly everything we threw their way.

As is so often the case, the weather gave us a brief respite around noon, just as our boat nosed onto the rocky shoreline at the southern end of the lake. Bucky had a plan in mind, and we hiked a short way across the mainland to where a small outlet of the lake catapulted over a six-metre cliff into an adjoining lake. As I peered over the edge into the tailwater below the falls, I watched with glee as first one, then another broad-shouldered brookie smugly lifted its nose out of the water and calmly engulfed an unsuspecting insect. Rising fish! I couldn't tell from my vantage point exactly what insect was enticing these fish to feed on the surface, but I quickly decided that in lieu of a "match the hatch" strategy, I'd simply offer them the largest, fattest-looking dry fly in my box. I tied on a #6 caddis imitation.

Clamouring down the rock face, I eased into the water well below the rising fish and began to strip out line in a series of false casts. I let my fly settle onto the surface once, well off-target from where the fish had been rising, as a means to accurately judge the length of line I had out. The big caddis plopped on the water like a floating Big Mac, and I quickly picked it up again, stripped out another two metres of line, then fired it into the current line above the first fish. It drifted about a metre before disappearing into the boiling vortex of a large, rising trout.

Eventually, after a worthy fight, the fish came to hand and I carefully slipped out the hook, admiring the shimmering colours as it slid back into the frigid water. It weighed about three pounds, but it wasn't the size of the fish that gave me pause nor the lack of same given where I was, rather that I'd enjoyed the privilege of taking such a gorgeous fish on a dry fly in a pristine landscape. Ten minutes later I had my second fish in hand, a carbon copy of the first. Then, as if on cue, the skies crackled, the wind picked up and the rain began to fall.

Weather kept the three of us cabin-bound for most of the next 24 hours, and our pilot eventually managed to get in to pick us up only by carefully hop-scotching his way from lake to lake under the low ceiling of clouds. We made it back to Kuujjuaq less than an hour before my flight back to Montréal was due to depart. There, in the tiny northern airport, I caught up with Mitch and Luke, and listened raptly as Luke related his successes catching lake trout back at Lake Gordon. I also got to hear the story of Neil's blackpowder caribou and the details of Susan's exciting stalk on the caribou she was cleaning when we left Gordon. It was a reunion of sorts, I guess, and a warm one. Friendships in hunting camps tend to be fleeting, and as we climbed aboard the 727 I acknowledged that although I'd likely never see these folks again, we'd made a strong connection in a short time. I know I'll think often of Luke.

As we climbed out leaving Kuujjuaq behind, I settled into my thoughts and became aware that for all the wonder and excitement it had offered, my time in the Ungava region had not satisfied the debt I owed myself. I'd arrived believing the trip would somehow satisfy my appetite for Québec's northernmost reaches, and that upon leaving I'd quickly uncover a new destination about which to dream. That's proven to be far from accurate. My time in the Ungava only served to whet my appetite for the rugged, remote and incredibly inspiring landscape. Apparently my conscience believes a little interest is due on that debt, and if going back is the only way to clear this marker from the books, then I guess I'm up for the task.

—ɷ—

15

THE BRUIN AND THE ROLLING STONES

I first got to know Jim Shockey when I was serving as editor for an upstart magazine and Jim came on as a regular columnist. In the ensuing years, I hunted out of his Vancouver Island bear camp on two occasions. In fact, I think I was the second or third hunter to take a bear with Jim after he began his outfitting business. Today, Jim is arguably the most well-known and well-respected hunter on the planet. Best of all, as a Saskatchewan native, he's one of our own. I generally only see Jim these days on the show circuit, and despite the many people and obligations seeking his attention, he always makes time to catch up. But that's Jim and one of his charms. Although he's ascended to the highest level of the worldwide hunting fraternity, he always has time for people, whether fans of his television shows or old acquaintances like me. Canadian hunters, and all ethical hunters worldwide, should be proud of how he represents us.

"**O**kay, who was the Beatles' original drummer?"

I pondered the question momentarily before responding with confidence, "That's easy, Pete Best."

"All right. Who played keyboards on albums for both the Beatles and the Rolling Stones?"

"Let me think about that one for a minute or two," replied bear outfitter and friend, Jim Shockey.

I was quite content to give Jim as much time as he needed, not just in the spirit of good sportsmanship, but also because my attention had been diverted by an enormous black shape slowly emerging from the thick tangle of alder alongside the ditch farther on down the road.

"There's one," I said matter of factly.

"Yeah, I see it," responded Jim, easing the truck ahead until we were only 100 metres or so away. "He's a good one, too, a definite shooter. I'd say he's easily in the 20 inch skull class, maybe better. Want to try and get him?"

"Hell, no," I countered. "We've only been hunting 20 minutes."

Jim just smiled, slowed the truck to a complete stop and said, "Good."

We were obviously thinking along the same lines. Despite the trophy quality of the mature boar black bear, it was far too early in the hunt to even consider filling my tag. We piled out of the truck and raised our binoculars, watching as the bear slowly made his way up the steep grade of the open hillside. He had all the trademark characteristics of a big bear—stubby-looking legs under a barrel-shaped body, wide spacing between his ears and a distinctive roly-poly waddle to his walk. He disappeared into an alder thicket, and we climbed back into the 4x4 to continue on down the road.

"I see you weren't just blowing smoke, Jim. You really do have some big bears in your neck of the woods," I offered, half in jest. "What do you figure that one would weigh?"

Jim grunted, then surmised, "I don't know. Close to four hundred pounds I'd guess…Billy Preston."

"What?" I asked, looking at Jim like he had four heads.

"The answer to your question, about the keyboard player I mean. It was Billy Preston."

The guy was sharp. Not only did he know his bears, but he obviously knew his music as well.

April on Vancouver Island was, as I had heard it would be, overwhelmingly beautiful, and I was enjoying every minute of it. A slight change in career path had left me some free time, and rather than sit around the house, complete my taxes or tackle any other equally mundane chore, I'd decided a road trip was in order. A whole "Me and You and a Dog Named Boo" kind of pilgrimage, with nothing but blue skies and the open road in my windshield. In no time at all, I was packed, and I do mean packed! My plan was to head to Vancouver Island for three or four weeks to see and do it all. I loaded up my saltwater, freshwater and fly-fishing gear. On top of that went my rifle and blackpowder gun, not to mention all the accessories no self-respecting hunter would be caught without. My shotgun is always packed, but I threw in a few extra boxes of light loads; a man can never tell when he might run into a sporting clays or skeet range. Then came sleeping bag, tent, cooler, stove and more. I wasn't going to abuse the opportunity by draining the household vacation account; I was going to travel cheap. Lastly, I made a few calls to people I knew on the Island to let them know I was on my way.

For those of you who think you might like to take a similar excursion someday, one of those "to hell with it, spur of the moment trips," I mean, let me offer you one piece of invaluable advice. You know all those friends, acquaintances and relatives you have? The ones who are always saying, "If you're ever out this way, give me a call. We'll go fishing." You know them—the ones who are just trying to be polite. Don't even give them the chance to say no. Just call and let them know what day you'll be there; tell them to gas up the boat and stock the bar with your favourite sippin' tea. Then tell them how much you're looking forward to seeing them and hang up the phone before they have a chance to stammer out a reply. It works beautifully. In just 15 minutes, I had booked more than three weeks of fun and relaxation, from salmon fishing to steelheading, and from trap shooting to kayaking.

One of the last calls I made was to Jim Shockey. Jim and I had known each other for a few years but had found little opportunity to spend time together. But he'd long amazed me with stories of the bears roaming around his guiding territory on northern Vancouver Island and had intimated that if I was ever out, I should try to find a few days to see it first-hand. Besides, I had once politely asked him to stop in for a whitetail hunt on his annual deer mission across the prairies, so I figured he had to return the favour. I quickly told Jim what days I'd be up his way, related as to how I could hardly wait, slammed down the phone and was on the highway. Just like that.

I really was looking forward to spending a few days chasing bruins with Jim. I've long enjoyed my spring bear hunts; they're the perfect remedy for pulling a non-ice-fisherman out of the cold weather blues. I was aware of the reputation Vancouver Island had earned for producing exceptional quality bears long before I'd met Jim, but this was going to be my first opportunity to see if that reputation was deserved.

I arrived in Port Hardy, Jim's spring home away from home, in the early afternoon and quickly located the motel where he put up his clients. Although Jim wasn't in, I enjoyed a welcoming chat with his guide before heading downtown. I figured I'd get my licence purchased and out of the way while I had time.

I had only just begun to wait in the interminably long line at the government agent's office when Jim strode in. Or should I say "Big Jim" as he cuts quite an imposing figure decked out in his guiding gear of cowboy boots, denims and a hat that would make Hoss Cartwright proud. We said our hellos, finished up the requisite paperwork and headed back to the motel. There I met the two hunters who were in camp. They were a jovial pair and rightly so because they'd seen many bears, and one of them had taken a 20-inch plus bear their second day. As it turned out, the other hunter tagged out the evening I arrived. As we still had about four hours of daylight left, Jim suggested we take a quick drive and see some country. We might even see a bear or two, he suggested.

We saw three bears that first evening, including that first one along the road. But neither of us was particularly interested in taking a bear right away. We were too busy enjoying the early spring weather and attempting to humiliate one another in our game of music trivia. I'm not really sure how it began, but we soon discovered that each of us had similar tastes in music and evenly matched, albeit competitive, minds (or lack thereof) when it came to music trivia. In any case, once it started there was no letting it go.

Over the next few days, when Jim would wake me in the morning, it wouldn't be with a cheery good morning but rather a challenging, "Okay, name two groups that Rod Stewart played with!"

"Geez, Jim," I'd reply, "The Faces and The Jeff Beck Group. Now let me sleep in peace for another half hour or so."

But I'd never go back to sleep. Like a 10-year old fooling his babysitter, I'd simply pretend to be asleep. In truth, I was plotting, scheming and dreaming up every uncelebrated fact about any obscure group or singer I could recall. There was no damn way I wasn't going to be prepared with an even tougher question each time Jim threw one my way.

On day two, Jim suggested that we go for a long drive because he wanted to check out a few areas in his territory he hadn't had the opportunity to visit yet. This was Jim's first year as owner of the outfitting territory, and he wanted to familiarize himself with it as quickly as possible. For those who aren't aware, in the province of BC, the rights to guiding territories are actually owned and can be subsequently sold at the whim of the current rightsholder. Jim was familiar with both the history and the potential of the black bear hunting on the northern half of Vancouver Island, and he didn't hesitate when the territory became available, deciding to make the leap from an antique business to pursue his true passion for hunting full time.

By mid-morning it was easy to see why Jim felt the way he did about the territory. We saw several bears just as we drove along the main road. And they were all big, mature animals. Jim explained that, as this was the early part of the season, the boars were up and moving, while the sows and cubs had yet to become active. In fact, in the three days I spent with Jim, I didn't see a single bear that wasn't, to our best judgment, a boar. They were all on their own and all trophy-class animals.

The bears on Vancouver Island grow big for the same reason that bears typically grow big anywhere—food and lots of it. The island's lush vegetation, rich berry crops and abundant marine and terrestrial animal life provide a smorgasbord of ursine delights that even Yogi himself would envy. Coupled with a favourable climate, relatively restricted access and limited hunting pressure, the area features an abundance of all the necessary ingredients for producing huge black bears and lots of them. It's easily defensible to suggest that Vancouver Island produces as many trophy class bears as anywhere on the continent. For the hardcore pursuer of bruins, however, it should be noted that there are no coloured bears here; they're all black with perhaps the odd splash of white thrown in here and there. But no brown, cinnamon or blonde bears.

Jim uses two distinctly different but equally effective methods when hunting spring bears. The first is a simple spot and stalk technique—cruising the logging roads, stopping to glass the cutover areas. Recent cutblocks warm up faster in the spring than do heavily timbered habitats, meaning new vegetation emerges there weeks before it starts growing in the cool of the shaded forest. Fresh grass and forb shoots are candy to spring bears, and they actively seek out these locations.

Any places where these roads come in close proximity to the ocean, particularly at the upper end of inlets, are another prime source of early spring bear food. Here it's the freshly greened salt grasses that attract them.

The other approach for locating bears Jim has found to be productive is to put his boat into the ocean and work the coastal inlets, again paying particular interest to the tidal flats where salt grasses emerge in early spring.

In either case, once a bear is located, the hunter attempts to stalk within a range that allows him or her to determine whether or not that particular bear is of shooting size. Judging bears is no simple matter; it's often best left to experienced guides, who look over several hundred bears each year. If a bear is of trophy size, the stalk continues in an attempt to get the hunter within effective shooting range. At the peak of the season, Jim says, it is not unusual for a hunter and his guide to look over 20 or more different bears each day.

As we continued on day two to look over some of the previously unexplored parts of Jim's territory, we stumbled on a road that appeared to wind its way south along the coast. We'd seen several bears by this time but hadn't made a serious play on any of them. The road doubled back on itself to get around a long inlet then started climbing back up into the timber. We stopped at the last break along the trail before the trees enclosed us once again, and we got out to glass the entire length of the inlet.

We both spotted the bear at the same time, almost a mile away and directly across the inlet from where we stood. He was slowly feeding his way upwind along the shore, selecting only the freshest and most lush vegetation to satisfy his palate. It was obvious at first glance that he was the kind of bear we were looking for, and we quickly decided to go after him.

After driving the truck to within a half-mile of where we'd last seen the bear, Jim leaned over and asked, "Blackpowder or the 7mm?"

"All I have with me this evening is the seven," I replied. "But if you have your smokepole handy, I'd be keen to try it."

"Absolutely. Here. Load it, and let's get going before that bear feeds his way back into the timber."

I took the gun from Jim and gripped it with the familiarity of an old friend. It was Modern Muzzleloader's MK-85 Predator in .50 cal., the same species of front stuffer I owned. I poured in a pre-measured load of Pyrodex, firmly seated the 310-grain sabotted lead bullet, capped it, made sure the weapon was on safe and nodded to Jim. Quickly but quietly we made our way down through the willow and alder to the shore, expecting to emerge about 90 metres from the bear. We poked our heads out and looked one way then the other. No bear.

"He probably kept feeding his way upwind," suggested Jim. "Follow me and be ready each time we round a bend."

With that, we set off at a quick but careful pace. Unfortunately, the sunlight was losing the same battle it wages daily with the forces of dusk; we didn't have a lot of legal light left.

I took three quick steps to stay tight to Jim, and three consecutive sounds erupted like machine gun fire from beneath the soles of my boots. Jim turned sharply with a look that said more than any words ever could. I shrugged my shoulders in meek apology and looked down. I had subconsciously been stepping from rock to rock, a tactic all flatland hunters use whenever practical to help reduce the noise resulting from our leaf and twig strewn landscapes. But here on the coast, the rocks are covered with fragments of broken clam and cockle shells. The smart move is to avoid the rocks, instead stepping into small clumps of tide-deposited vegetation where the moisture content mutes any possible noise. How was I to know?

We continued down the shore for a couple hundred metres, expecting at every bend to come upon the bruin. But he'd apparently vanished as bears are wont to do, so we turned into the shrubbery and started making our way toward the trail for the short hike back to the vehicle. We emerged onto the trail shoulder to shoulder and instantly froze. There, not 40 metres away, was our bear. We'd found one of the island's truly massive bears; this mature boar looked to top the scales at over 400 pounds, with a thick, luxurious black coat and a broad, heavy skull. I quickly raised the rifle, but the sudden movement alerted the bear to our presence. He swung his head our way just as I found the spot behind his shoulder through the scope. I squeezed the trigger, and through the smoky air that hung on the end of the barrel watched as the bear wheeled in place, ran up a six-metre rise and disappeared into the darkness of the dense coastal forest.

Jim and I looked at one another, our faces and minds mirroring each other's perfectly. We'd have to go into the thick stuff to sort out a wounded bear. We agreed that the shot had looked good, probably going through both lungs and out the other side. Chances were good that the bear wouldn't be too far. Jim went back to the truck and grabbed his .300 Weatherby, just in case, while I rearmed the muzzleloader. Together we scrambled up the short but steep slope and prepared to step into the nearly impenetrable forest where the bear had vanished. And I do mean impenetrable. It was clear that we were going to have to make our way on hands and knees in many places. Darkness was closing fast, and neither of us relished the task at hand.

"One last thing," Jim murmured softly.

"What's that?" I asked, expecting some last-minute sage advice from the seasoned bear hunter and outfitter.

"What's the last name of a Canadian singer who goes by the name of Garfield? This is for all the marbles."

I couldn't believe my ears. I mean, here we were, getting ready to shake hands with a huge black bear, who is wounded I might add; our light is disappearing noticeably with each passing second; and this guy's still trying to play Stump the Band. And with a dirty, rotten, unfair question to boot. I don't think Jim quite understands the difference between trivia and trivial!

I shook my head in mock disgust and pushed Jim into the darkness of the timber. After all, I reasoned, he's the guide. He should go first. We hadn't made it 25 metres into the dense understory when an unnatural sound caught our attention. We squinted in the direction from where it appeared to originate and instantly locked eyes onto a mass of unruly, jet black hair. Our bear was facing us, about 15 metres away and down but clearly not wanting to stay that way. He was snapping his jaws, waving his front paws and growling in obvious frustration. You didn't have to be Dr. Doolittle to know this bruin was mad and wanted to express his feelings in a more direct way. I wasn't about to wait to find out if the old adage that "where there's a will, there's a way" holds true for bears; I took two steps to the side and fired. This quieted the bruin, though I reloaded and shot once more just to be sure.

We shook hands in congratulations, and Jim went off to fetch the truck. Fortunately, we could get it to within 50 metres of where the bear lay, but it took the two of us the best part of an hour to get him out of the trees and up into the truck. It was too dark by this time for skinning, and we wanted to get some photos in the morning light, so we started the two-hour drive for camp.

A few minutes down the road, Jim turned to me and said, "Geez, Ken, you're pretty quiet. Thinking about going in to the thick stuff after that bear, eh?"

"Not at all, Jim," I answered, "I'm thinking about the absurd level of competitiveness it must take to ask that last trivia question. I mean, come on, talk about obscure. That's ridiculous!"

"Yeah, I know," said Jim admittedly, starting to apologize. I cut him off before he could finish.

"Anyway, the answer is French, Garfield French," I spat out smugly. Jim turned as white as a ghost, sputtering in astonishment. "I saw him while I was at university in Guelph in 1976," I continued. "Kinda liked their music, but they broke up just a few years later. I thought I was about the only person who'd ever heard of them, much less could remember them. I can't believe you asked me that question."

Jim didn't say much the rest of the way home, and the next morning woke me with a very pleasant, " Good morning, Ken. Looks like a beautiful day out there."

—⋙—

16

THE JEWEL OF JASPER

Jim Mitchell and I have hunted and fished together for more than 25 years. He spent many years in the corporate world as a highly placed executive in the construction field, but always preferred the outdoor life to that of the big city. Jim is one of those individuals who seems to know everybody, but I could always count on him when I was looking for a fishing or hunting partner. Over the years, we've travelled together often and always had a great time along the way. He was a regular fixture at my fall duck and deer camp for a long time. One of those types who could fix or build darn near anything, he willingly helped whenever a camp expansion or repair was needed. As expected, when he retired Jim moved to the country, so I don't see him as much as I once did. When we do get together, however, it's still generally with rod or rifle in hand.

When Jasper National Park comes to mind for most people, including avid anglers, their thoughts usually turn to world-class skiing, abundant wildlife and breathtaking scenery. And rightfully so because Jasper has all these features in spades. Seldom do many associate Jasper with fishing. I know I didn't. Until I had the opportunity to cast a line there, that is.

An invitation to join a bunch of the boys for a weekend of golf, fishing and poker at Jasper came my way early one summer. Frankly, I'm not enough of a golfer to justify that amount of time and expense just to chase a ball around, regardless of how awe-inspiring the scenery might be. And the chance to take home a few quarters from these lifetime members of the "Easy Money School of Gambling" wasn't challenge enough to get me to search my pockets for loose change, much less go to the trouble of preparing for a weekend campout. But fishing a new lake? Now, that was a reason to go!

To tell the truth, I've never been all that enthralled with fishing trout in lakes; I much prefer moving water and have always been a little unsure of myself (read "lousy at it") when it comes to tackling still-water rainbows. But the boys were thinking ahead and booked Lorne Currie and his guiding service for our first day on the water, totally changing the scenario. Lorne is a legend in these parts. At one time he owned and operated a tackle shop in Jasper and has been guiding in the park for more years than he'd probably care to remember. If I was ever going to learn the secrets to fishing these challenging waters, it would be with Lorne.

Our day with Lorne dawned bright, clear and cool—perfect fishing conditions. Those of us who had chosen to fish for the day grabbed a quick bite and hopped into our vehicles for the 50-kilometre drive to Maligne Lake. Maligne is, in a word, stunning. None of the calendars or postcards do justice to the magnificence of this landscape—clear, blue-green water reflecting a backdrop of dark alpine forests and rugged, snow-capped mountain peaks. With each passing mile, I was becoming increasingly anxious to wet a line.

Maligne is the largest lake in Jasper, some 22 kilometres long and nearly 100 metres deep. Her waters are cold, rarely rising above 15 degrees Celsius, and like most glacier-fed alpine lakes, relatively unproductive. The lake's aquatic insect populations and the creatures that feed on them, including the fish species, are associated almost exclusively with the lake bottom near to shore or in water less than 4.5 metres deep. It's only in the relatively shallow water of this littoral zone that sunlight sustains the plant communities that form the foundation for higher life forms. For this reason, most of the best fishing waters in many high-country lakes can be reached from shore. The advantage of boats in a large lake such as Maligne is simply improved access to all sections of the lakeshore and the ease of casting they facilitate.

In the low productivity waters of cold, alpine lakes, food abundance and availability is generally the limiting factor to the growth of fish. In lakes with little forage, growth rates can be agonizingly slow. As an example, 12-year-old rainbow trout from Upper Jade Lake in Mt. Revelstoke National Park can weigh less than 10 ounces, and a four-year old rainbow out of Lower Jade Lake weighed in at a mere 2.8 ounces! At the other end of the scale, a rainbow trout out of one of the more productive Valley of the Five Lakes reached 20 pounds at less than 10 years of age. Maligne Lake lies somewhere in the middle with respect to growth rates; average fish will tip the scales between one and three pounds. Five- and six-pound fish are taken with some regularity, though much larger fish are present. In fact, Alberta's record brook trout, at 12 pounds 14 ounces, comes from Maligne, as does the record rainbow trout that tipped the scales at a staggering 20 pounds 4 ounces.

As luck would have it, I got a seat in Lorne's boat, along with friend and trip organizer Jim Mitchell. Two other boats, each with two anglers and a guide, joined us. While the others were fishing with conventional tackle, Jim, Lorne and I chose to test our luck with fly gear. The boat that carried us across the lake was downright beautiful—a handsome, square-sterned cedar-strip canoe that Lorne had built himself. Gasoline-powered engines are not permitted on Maligne, but the battery-powered trolling motors pushed our sleek craft effortlessly through the gin-clear waters.

Heading south from the dock, stopping only briefly to try our luck in a few bays, Lorne piloted us toward one of his favourite hotspots. As we travelled, Lorne talked tackle and techniques, pausing only to identify the towering peaks above us with their familiar names, including Mount Charlton, Maligne Mountain, Mount Paul and Mount Henry MacLeod. High on the southwest faces of a few of the peaks, we could make out the gleaming white coats of mountain goats as they fed on the rich grasses of avalanche chutes. Along the shore, a cow moose lifted her head momentarily to stare back as we glided past before serenely lowering it to continue feeding. We were enjoying a magnificent day and had yet to even get serious about fishing.

Maligne Lake boasts two prominent target species—rainbow and brook trout. Both are stocked strains of fish. While there are some native Athabasca rainbows in Jasper, they are confined to a select few of the park's streams. Brookies were first introduced to the Maligne system in 1928, and along with rainbows, were bred and developed for introduction into park waters at a hatchery in Jasper until 1972. The hatchery was closed that year, in part because of a viral infection that had been discovered, in part because of unsatisfactory success in stocking some of the high-mountain lakes and in part simply because of changing national park policy. For Maligne, the closure was insignificant; the rainbows and brookies are both self-sustaining populations, spawning successfully every year.

We finally arrived in the area where we would do most of our fishing and slowed to trolling speed. Jim and Lorne both tied on nymph patterns that imitated the lake's freshwater shrimp, a preferred food source for trout in these waters. I tied on a Doc Spratley, a small streamer fly common to most fly-fishermen. We let out our lines and slowly cruised the underwater cut-offs adjacent to shore in a long "S" pattern. Lorne advised that we let out the entirety of our fly lines when trolling, as in these clear waters fish spook easily. It wasn't long before Jim let out a holler, and a silvery rainbow broke the surface in a spectacular tail-walk some 30 metres behind the boat. After an entertaining fight, Lorne carefully netted the two-pound 'bow, and Jim held it aloft for the obligatory photos before returning it to its icy refuge.

Over the next hour, Jim landed another rainbow while Lorne boated a brookie and a rainbow, all in the two-pound class. I continued to be held off the score sheet, much to the smirking delight of my two boatmates. I finally gave in to Lorne's suggestion and reeled in so that he could tie on one of his secret shrimp-imitating patterns. I thanked him and returned my line to the water. Almost immediately I had a hit, and leaned firmly back to set the hook. There was brief resistance then nothing. I'd lost the fish. Oh well, I figured that I was at least in the game now and settled back, ready for the next strike. It didn't come. Meanwhile, Jim and Lorne each boated another couple fish, one a beautiful three-pound brookie.

I retained my patience, figuring that with three identical flies trailing through the water it was just a matter of luck that my time would soon come. But the next hit was on Jim's line again, and when he offered me the opportunity to play the fish with near textbook condescension and a grin like that of the cat who'd swallowed the proverbial canary, I briefly considered throwing him overboard. As he fought to land the chrome-plated rainbow, he and Lorne giggled themselves silly at my plight. I don't take an old-fashioned whippin' lightly and quickly reeled in. I was determined to go back to a fly of my own choosing and teach both of these guys a thing or two about fishing.

I couldn't have been more shocked when I got my line back to the boat only to discover I was fishing without a fly! The first, and only, fish that had hit my offering had taken my fly with him. I'd been trolling around Maligne Lake with no lure for nearly an hour! With so much line out, there is no difference in felt resistance between a line with a fly and one without, so I had no way of knowing. But talk about your rookie mistakes; mine was about as dumb as they get! There is no place to hide out on the water, so I just ducked my head while the two of them buried me under a fusillade of wisecracks. Their laughs shook the canoe so violently I thought we'd capsize for sure. Eventually, their howls turned to guffaws and finally to snickers, and I ultimately found the courage to lift my head to tie on a new fly.

Grabbing the end of my leader, the tell-tale curly remains jumped out at me. While I had been too bone-headed to think about checking my fly for an hour, I hadn't tied it on in the first place. Lorne had! And that fish hadn't broken me off; the knot had slipped. Lorne's knot! Lorne, our guide! The one who'd nearly laughed me out of his boat! I didn't have to say a word, I merely held up the end of the line for all to see. Jim started howling again; Lorne turned red; and I just smiled and shook my head, unsure whether to laugh or cry.

Eventually, we all got back to fishing and had a truly wonderful time. I caught my share of fish, and we joined up with the others for a mouth-watering shore lunch and a chance to swap lies. The others had enjoyed an even better morning than we had in terms of numbers of fish caught. That wasn't unexpected because they were using the tried and true technique of trolling a flasher tied about two metres in front of a single hook baited with a worm. For the hardware fisherman, there is no better offering.

Our afternoon was as productive as the morning, and at day's end we hit the dock with full hearts to match our full bellies. Seldom have I enjoyed a day's fishing more, and I'd discovered that Jasper isn't only for snow bunnies showing off the latest in après-ski fashions or for camera-clad tourists taking photos of Grandma in front of the mountain scenery. Jasper, and Maligne Lake in particular, offers the fishermen searching for solitude, tranquility and spectacular angling one of his last refuges.

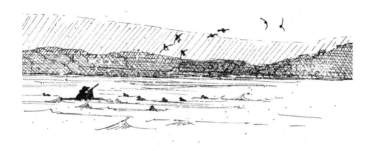

17

GETTING THAT OLD SINKING FEELING

Sinkboxes harken back to an earlier time when they were a popular and highly successful method for hunting waterfowl. Although as effective as ever, they're seldom used these days. Québec's Lac Saint-Pierre is one of the last places in Canada you'll still find them in regular use. I have a strong affection for the traditions of waterfowling, and it was a desire to recapture a lost time that led me to spend a couple days neck-deep in the St. Lawrence River.

Freezing spray blankets the nape of my neck like a million tiny needles, and I hunch up in response, pulling the collar of my parka up and the back flap of my hat down. It does little good; however, as the next surge washes over me, forcing me to shake off, retriever-like, the excess water before it freezes to my clothing. With the waves steadily increasing in size, I grab the ratchet and crank up the sinkbox an inch or two, trying desperately to give myself a little more freeboard against the rising water levels. I wonder momentarily just what the hell I'm doing here but find myself smiling as I recall that this was all my idea...against the better judgment of those who know better.

The idea of hunting waterfowl from a sinkbox intrigued me for years. I'm fascinated by the history of waterfowl gunning in North America, and sinkboxes are definitely an anachronism in the modern waterfowling world of spinning-wing decoys, layout blinds and tungsten shot. For those not familiar, a sinkbox is the aquatic equivalent of a pit blind. Designed to accommodate one or two shooters, it's little more than a steel box countersunk into a floating wooden platform. Hunters shooting from a sinkbox sit with their shoulders near water level, making them all but invisible to incoming birds, especially if there's any chop on the water.

Although legal across most of Canada, the St. Lawrence River is one of the few remaining areas where sinkbox hunting continues to thrive. Historically, sinkboxes were used predominantly by market gunners, not by sportsmen, with 300-duck days, or more, regularly described in the literature. Although cumbersome and heavy, sinkboxes were extremely effective if taking large numbers of waterfowl was your sole objective, as was the case when restaurant demand for wild duck meat was high. They were so effective that the use of sinkboxes was prohibited in New York State as far back as 1838. While the market gunners of the day adhered to the prohibition for a short time, they considered the law an infringement on their rights and an impairment of their ability to earn a living. Eventually, they took to their sinkboxes again, wearing masks to conceal their identity and threatening those who might expose them. At some point, sinkboxes became accepted once again; the law was no longer enforced and was eventually repealed.

During the market gunning era, sinkboxes were most commonly referred to as "batteries." And while there can be no doubting their effectiveness, equally true is the potential danger to which hunters were exposed when gunning from them. On the big bays of the eastern seaboard, weather fronts can arise in the blink of an eye, and a hunter whose tender boat was too far away to respond quickly could easily find himself in danger of sinking. As the literature relates, more than a few hunters lost their lives when caught in foul weather, their sinkbox becoming little more than an iron coffin. Fortunately, today's sinkboxes have the benefit of modern materials and design technology, and as a result, are much safer and more stable. That knowledge, however, was of little comfort to me as I braced against another wave breaking over the sloping surface of my sinkbox platform. It was November 30, and the local weather was doing nothing to belie the climatic inferences of the calendar.

After several years of thinking about a sinkbox hunt, I finally made the leap and called Lac Saint-Pierre Outfitters to inquire about openings. Unfortunately, our respective calendars left few openings that worked; the only time that suited us both was the last few days in November. They were up-front in cautioning that consistent waterfowling could be all but over that late in the year, ultimately dependent upon how the birds responded to whatever the late season weather brought. I was hell-bent on the idea by that time; however, and agreed to take my chances. I was much more interested in the experience of sinkbox hunting than I really was in shooting large numbers of ducks.

Lac Saint-Pierre is, in reality, no lake at all but a natural widening of the St. Lawrence River. Stretching 40 kilometres long by 24 kilometres wide, it encompasses more than 13,000 hectares of channels and marshes that attract staging and migrating waterfowl by the thousands each fall. Inland and shoreline marshes offer superb gunning for a variety of dabbler species, including mallards and black ducks along with significant numbers of snow geese. On the open water, where the sinkboxes are used, canvasbacks, redheads and bluebills are the preferred and most abundant targets. The timing of my hunt meant that most of those species were already bound for warmer climes, but the hardy goldeneye were likely to still be around. They were what we'd be after.

Sinkbox hunting, like most waterfowling, is an early morning affair at its best, and my first of two days saw me up at 5:00 AM for a quick but filling breakfast before meeting my guide, Andre. Andre spoke little, and when he did it was in broken English, but he had the stoic look particular to so many experienced guides and hunters. His eyes were confident and his movements sure, giving me great assurance that if anybody could find ducks this late in the season, he could. The ride to the hunting grounds took 40 minutes in the 18-foot fiberglass boat customized for duck hunting duty with wooden wells built along both sides to store decoys. It was bitterly cold and pitch dark when we set out, only a pencil-thin silhouette of dark vegetation separating the water from the sky. Islands loomed suddenly out of the darkness like ocean-going freighters, but Andre's deftness on the tiller combined with his thorough knowledge of the local waters soon eased any worries I might have. As the light grew, so too did the breeze, and the skeletons of leafless cottonwoods and willows waved to us as we zipped past. Twenty minutes in, I could no longer tell if the water falling on us was rain or the spray from our boat, but the sting of freezing water droplets convinced me to turn and lower my head. With each passing minute, the weather grew progressively worse, and eventually, I began to question my sanity. So, too, I suspect did Andre, but his resolute stare told me he was all business. I found confidence in that.

Eventually, we moved away from the shoreline and the islands, crossing open water. We could see waterfowl in the distance rise in spiraling vortexes, their movements barely discernible, clouds of dark shapes against a slate gray backdrop. We finally arrived at the sinkbox, a mile offshore, and tethered it to the tender boat. After towing it for another half-mile or so, we stopped. Andre and I clambered onto the slippery deck of the platform, where he flipped the upright box portion into the cavity of the deck before ratcheting it into place with long threaded bolts on each side. We dropped an anchor off each end to secure the blind in place, and I climbed down into the box while Andre jumped back into the tender boat and began setting out the decoys. He dropped five dozen beautifully hand-crafted goldeneye blocks around the blind, tied in tandem, before waving to me and heading off into the growing light of the morning sky. He anchored about a half-mile away, just close enough that he'd be able to see if I dropped any birds without being close enough to alarm them. Should I shoot any birds, he'd motor in and retrieve them right away because downed birds can drift a long way quickly in the current and winds of the St. Lawrence.

On my own, I settled in and appraised my surroundings. The blind platform was about five metres long by two metres wide with the steel box sunk in the middle, and we'd anchored in about five metres of water. To minimize hunter movement, the two-man box is tight with a cushion on the steel bench offering a modicum of comfort and a small shelf for shells. My shoulders were at water level, and it's an eerie feeling to know most of you is well below the water's surface. The morning was monochromatic, and it was difficult to separate the olive-gray water from the overcast gray sky, much less discern any detail. Hundreds upon hundreds of two-foot square chunks of ice bumped their way through the decoys, harbingers of the layer of river ice that would form any day.

The birds weren't flying much that day; over the morning, I saw several small flights of goldeneye, a couple handfuls of scaup, a few scoters and a pair of mergansers. I could easily have taken the mergansers, but opted not to shoot anything I'd rather not eat. Three scaup, my favourite of all duck species, managed to sneak in right on top of me while I was focused on a flight of goldeneye, and they escaped without so much as a feather ruffled.

I had to fight to remain warm and focused. Chipping away sheets of ice from where they formed on the metal of the box, the soles of my boots and on my parka offered a welcome diversion. A few cargo ships passed by in the main channel to the south. My imagination had me wondering if I was in any danger of being run over or swamped, but common sense told me I was well outside the shipping lanes. About noon, I waved to Andre in the tender boat; the birds had stopped flying, and there was little sense in just sitting out there getting colder. Back at the lodge, I could tell Guy was feeling concerned about the limited shooting I'd experienced, but I assured him I'd been well warned about the prospects at this time of year and had thoroughly enjoyed the morning, despite the limited shooting opportunities. I've shot more than my share of ducks over the years, and I was here to absorb the experience of hunting from a sinkbox. Limit shoots weren't what I was after. Nonetheless, we hoped the forecasted improvement in the weather for the next day would see more birds in the air.

As predicted, day two started with much more moderate weather, but by the time I was settled into the box, the wind and waves were picking up again. With the river's current going in one direction and the wind in opposition, the waves were quickly stacking up pretty high and were soon crashing over the platform's deck. As the minutes turned to hours, the weather continued to worsen. I could have waved for Andre at any time, probably should have, but in some absurd way I was enjoying the experience. I wasn't about to quit until I'd had my fill. Eventually, as water continued to pour over the top and the risk of being flooded out became increasingly real, I had to crank the sinkbox up a few inches. With the box sitting a little higher, waves breaking over the platform disappeared harmlessly through the gap between the platform and the box itself, which was suspended in the centre. Soon, however, the still-building waves overcame this meager defense, and again, water began to fill up the box around my feet. I could have raised the box again but reckoned that a higher profile would defeat the whole purpose of shooting from a sinkbox. Besides, it was apparent that the birds wouldn't be flying in the storm. Quite frankly, it didn't make much sense for anything to be moving about that didn't have to.

I sat in the sinkbox, lurching about in the turbulent water, for four hours that morning. I was cold, very cold, and it was only my high-tech waterfowling gear that prevented me from getting soaked to the skin from head to toe. The largest of the waves actually sent sprays of water completely over my head, but I'd grown quite confident in the sturdiness of my little metal home even in the midst of that vast piece of water. At one point, I found myself actually laughing out loud at the absurdity of it all. I mean it was pretty clear I wouldn't be shooting any ducks that day, but I really had no desire to be anywhere other than where I was. The words of renowned waterfowling writers like Heilner, Walsh and Reiger echoed in my mind, and I imagined myself as these men had described the market hunters of yesteryear. But times have changed, and after a last steely-eyed squint through the splash and spray,

I reluctantly waved for Andre. The romanticism of the sink-box had long disappeared for him, I'm sure, and it wasn't fair to keep him out in this weather any longer just so I could continue to live out a fantasy.

I had to fly home that night, but before leaving the lodge I made it clear that I'd be back. From my perspective, the hunting experience had been everything I'd wanted and more. They, on the other hand, wanted me to experience first-hand the otherworldly gunning opportunities hunters enjoy through the relatively mild weather of September and October when limit shoots on some mornings can be measured in minutes. I'll enjoy that opportunity when it comes, no doubt, but I can't imagine that the experience of a sinkbox hunt will ever be quite the same for me again.

18

PELEE ISLAND—WHERE RINGNECKS REIGN

Native to China, ring-necked pheasants are one of the few introduced game species that have captured the hearts and minds of Canadian sportsmen. Their appearance is both distinctive and beautiful; they're challenging to hunt and fabulous on the table. And I suppose it's those characteristics that have made them a favourite with wingshooters for nearly a century. I've hunted them regularly in my home province of Alberta, but this was the first time I left the Wild Rose province to pursue them. My experience served to confirm that, as in real estate, location is everything.

That first shot is always the most important, your chance to set the tone. When hunting in a new place with people you don't know, there's a certain pressure to prove your mettle, to show you deserve the privilege of hunting their grounds. And it's not meet-the-parents nervousness. It's more like the-jury-is-back anxiety.

Fortunately, I had little time to be anxious when that first cackling Pelee Island pheasant launched from cover about 30 metres out. Reacting on pure instinct, I shouldered my shotgun, pushed the stacked barrels out in front of the crossing bird and hit the switch. The rooster crumpled mid-air and had barely tumbled back to the ground before he was firmly in the grasp of the Labrador that had rousted him from his hideaway.

It was the first flush, and I'd passed the test. Of course, as the rest of that day and the next revealed, I was more than capable of missing "gimme" shots, but nothing settles the nerves like getting out of the gate without stumbling…especially when you're on a fabled, bucket-list hunt like this.

Think of Ontario's Pelee Island, and it's likely that award-winning wines from the venerable Pelee Island Winery come to mind. But if you're an avid upland bird hunter, you're probably also aware of this tiny island's annual pheasant hunt—an award winner in its own right as I discovered.

Pelee is unique by many standards. A two-hour ferry ride from Leamington or nearby Kingsville, it is the largest island in Lake Erie. At only 41 square kilometres, it's small from a hunting perspective. It's also the southernmost populated place in Canada, its latitude equivalent to that of northern California. As such, the climate is among the mildest in the country. Taking advantage, a wine industry arose in the 1860s, collapsed in the early 1900s then rose to prominence again in the 1980s.

There are only about 300 year-round residents but roughly 1200 seasonal inhabitants, including renowned Canadian author Margaret Atwood. A revered destination in birdwatching circles with a reputation for hosting superb annual arts and music festivals, Pelee outpunches its weight on the tourism front. Within the hunting community, however, the island is lionized for its annual Pelee Island Pheasant Hunt.

Ringnecks were first introduced in the 1890s with the inaugural hunt held in 1932. All these decades later, the island remains a bucket-list destination for those wanting to soak up the quaint, small-town atmosphere while revelling in the outstanding hunting. The locals are fully behind the hunt, from the "Welcome Hunters" banner hanging at the town hall to the regulations allowing hunters to hunt almost anywhere on the island without having to first seek permission from property owners. There's even a sign reading "Warning. No Hunting School Zone" alongside the township's only school, a reminder to enthusiastic hunters to keep common sense about them.

Aside from grapes, the primary crops on the agriculturally dominated landscape are soybeans, wheat and corn. A quick drive around reveals the island is a matrix of open fields, hedgerows, vineyards and thick tree and brush cover, making for ideal pheasant habitat and more than enough challenge for hunters to keep it all interesting.

On my Pelee Island hunt, I was accompanied by *Outdoor Canada* publisher Mark Yelic and editor-in-chief Patrick Walsh for the third of three annual two-day hunts. The Township of Pelee releases 4500 pheasants every Monday and Tuesday for three successive weeks, giving the birds ample time to distribute and settle in before the hunts take place on the Thursday and Friday. The township does an excellent job of rearing these birds, as demonstrated by the fact that, despite hunting with five dogs, only one bird was trapped on our hunts. All the others flushed and flew like the wildest of ringnecks.

Our host for the hunt, Kyle Davis, is the township's environmental services manager and an avid hunter and angler. Accompanying him were three friends, and along with Kyle's Lab, we had their two Nova Scotia duck tollers and two German short-haired pointers to do the heavy lifting.

Regulations dictate that the hunt begins at 8:00 AM, and on day one we were dutifully parked beside our chosen field with time for a coffee before heading out. As no further permission is required, access to a particular property is determined on a first-come, first-served basis. You simply park beside the field you want to hunt, and that is honoured by the other groups.

Each day's kickoff is an event unto itself. If you recall the opening sequence of *Saving Private Ryan*, you'll have some idea of what it sounded like at 8:01 AM on our first morning. From all corners of the island, we heard shooting, testament to the hunter-to-bird ratio. Each gunner is permitted 10 pheasants over two days, but it matters little whether you shoot them all the first morning or take the full two days.

There clearly must have been some low-hanging pheasants, because after the initial volley, the shooting petered out to a regular but more expected level. Just a few minutes in, one of Kyle's friends clobbered our group's first bird, a rooster going straight away with an eager pointer on its tail. Then I managed to drop my first bird, that crossing rooster. And just like that, we were into birds with everyone's focus, including that of the dogs, on high alert.

It's considered bad form in the business world to beat your boss in a game of golf; doing so can lead to unexpectedly finding yourself on the must-go list in the next round of downsizing. In my world, shooting is equivalent to golf, so it was with some trepidation that I accepted the invitation to join Mark and Patrick on this hunt. I mean, what would happen to my writing gig if I was to outshoot them by any significant margin?

As it turned out, I needn't have worried. On that first morning, they both proved to be at least as proficient as I was with the new Berettas we were field testing. Although each of us gassed a couple we should have made—as can be expected when targeting deceptively fast-flying pheasants—Kyle and his crew thankfully picked up the slack.

Even when pheasants abound, they're incredibly adept at finding unexpected places to hide, so we had to be constantly at the ready and quick on the trigger as we moved from cover to cover. By day's end, we had 33 birds in hand, plenty of kilometres on our boots and pockets brimming with spent shells. We'd definitely earned every bird in the bag.

The Pelee Island Pheasant Hunt is well organized as you might expect from an event with such a long and storied history. The township provides maps of the island, including the primary pheasant release locations, along with a list of available accommodations. There is only one hotel on the island but no shortage of cottages for rent, as well as bed and breakfasts.

To participate, hunters must preregister and purchase a special licence. The capacity for each two-day hunt is 600 hunters, but recently the average has been between 300 and 400, so there's a remarkable amount of terrain to choose from. Over our two days, we only once bumped into a hunter from another party. To add a little excitement to the mix, two banded roosters are released each week; shoot one and you receive a complimentary licence for the following year's hunt. We met a group that had bagged one, and they were rightfully thrilled.

On Pelee, the birds are widely dispersed and the cover unimaginably thick, making the hunt unlike any other released-pheasant hunt I've experienced. We began our second morning's hunt on a property managed by the Nature Conservancy of Canada and had to push our way through knee-high cover that would wear you out if you didn't take the occasional break. That afternoon we were all but lost in a sea of doghair-thick brush that left more than one of our crew muttering expletives in frustration.

But it is the thick stuff the birds move to after they realize the game is afoot, so if you want to put them up, you have little choice but to go in after them. When we did flush a bird in heavy cover, we had but a fleeting moment to shoulder and swing before it disappeared from sight. Finding downed birds also proved to be a chore on occasion, even with the assistance of the competent dogs. But challenge is welcome, if not expected, and by nearly every standard the

Pelee experience matches or exceeds the best pheasant hunting to be found anywhere.

I can't recall exactly how many birds we shot that second day, but it was somewhere in the neighbourhood of 25, bringing our two-day total to about 60. That's a lot of pheasants to take care of, but in true entrepreneurial fashion, some island residents have established a cleaning service. We were able to get our birds cleaned, packed and frozen for the trip home.

It's a funny thing, but bird hunters seldom recall many of the individual birds they shoot. Invariably, our strongest memories are of the places we hunt and the people we meet along the way. The evening after our second hunt, in a gracious gesture, Kyle invited us to his home, where in traditional après-hunt fashion we chowed down on shore-caught walleye fillets, poured back a few sundowners, laughed good-naturedly about each other's misses and recalled memorable retrieves.

I don't know when I'll get back to Pelee Island for another pheasant hunt, but I certainly didn't scratch it off my bucket list when I got home.

—∿∿—

19

BACK IN THE SADDLE

Alberta's Rocky Mountain foothills were long acclaimed as one of the finest destinations for elk. Over time, however, habitat alteration and improved access, increased predator populations and a host of other influences have contributed to a significant decline in eastern slopes elk populations. These days, much of the best elk hunting can be found in regions where large tracts of forested land abut agriculture; the combination of secure cover and abundant, nutrient-rich food allows elk to thrive. Saddle Hills County is one of those areas.

I stand frozen, afraid to even twitch; only my eyes move. Somewhere to my south is a bull elk. I know he's less than 100 metres away because I could feel his last challenging whistle reverberate up my spine. North of me is another rut-stirred bull. He, too, has betrayed his location with an equally blood-curdling bugle. Judging by the sound, he's even closer, likely less than 60 metres away. Yet no matter how hard I squint through the thick mixed-wood forest, I can't see either bull. Next to me, standing equally statue-like, bow in hand, is guide Logan Dolen. Knowing the elk are nearly in our laps and closing ground but not being able to see them makes the scenario all the more exhilarating.

The forest suddenly goes deathly quiet as if all of nature is holding its breath in anticipation of what will happen next. It's a game of chicken. Unfortunately, Dolen and I blink first, unable to withstand the suspense any longer. We take just one step forward, in unison, and the immediate crashing of trees to the northwest causes us to turn in time to make out the antlers of a huge bull as he storms away through the brush, a mere 30 metres distant.

As if choreographed, similar sounds erupt south of us a second later, a signal the other bull has also recognized our trap and is exiting furiously stage right. Dolen and I look at each other, our faces betraying an odd mix of awe and disappointment, before breaking out in laughter. The jig is up, at least for today. But the excitement of being up close and personal with two mature bull elk is more than worth the frustration of knowing our impatience blew the opportunity. That's elk hunting in a nutshell, but here in northwest Alberta's Saddle Hills County we know more opportunity awaits.

To fully understand just what an outdoorsperson's paradise Saddle Hills County has become requires you to step back in time 100 years to when the area was first being settled. The Edmonton, Dunvegan and British Columbia Railway opened up much of Alberta's Peace River region for settlement, but on its completion in 1916, the rail line had completely ignored the area that is now Saddle Hills County. Partly as a result of the failure to include the county in the rail line, today, a mere 2200 residents are spread across the county's 5800 square kilometres with no cities, towns or villages to be found. The largest cluster of people, in fact, is huddled in the hamlet of Woking, which boasts only 100 residents.

By some measure, I suppose, the region never reached its full potential. But if your vision of paradise includes vast tracts of native forests and numerous cool rivers and creeks with few people and limited agricultural, forestry and petroleum activity, then Saddle Hills County is a must-visit destination. For outdoorspeople, there can be few more appealing places.

It had been 20 years since I'd last hunted the Saddle Hills. Back then, I was after whitetails and mule deer, but the abundance and diversity of big game I saw there left a deep impression on me. So, when the opportunity arose to return to hunt rutting elk with well-known outfitter Mike Ukrainetz, it was simply too appealing to pass up. While I'd never hunted with Mike, I'd known him for many years, and his reputation for providing a first-class hunting experience was no secret.

I arrived at the lodge early on a mid-September afternoon. The timing was perfect, with the local elk sure to be fully into the rut. Camp was near deserted when I pulled in as all of Mike's guides and hunters were in the field, many of them hunting elk while others pursued moose, mule deer or whitetails.

By the time I'd settled in and grabbed a bite to eat, they started to return full of stories of exciting morning hunts. As is typical in big game camps, especially early in the fall when the days are long, most of the hunters headed to their rooms for a nap after a hearty lunch. In the meantime, the guides attended to the never-ending chores that make their three-month guiding season an exercise in stamina.

It was 6:00 PM before I headed out with Dolen, a 20-something local whose family farms in the county. Guiding isn't Dolen's primary occupation, even through the fall months; he only guides for Mike when an extra hand is needed in camp. The fact that Dolen wasn't a full-time guide didn't concern me in the least. From our first conversation, it was clear he was a hunter through and through with the focused mind of a predator. And given he was a local resident, I was confident he knew the lay of the land and local game movements as well as or better than any guide from outside the county could.

Mid-September anywhere at this latitude is resplendent in fall colours, but never more so than here in the Peace River valley. It's difficult not to be mesmerized by the kaleidoscope of colours that greet you as you travel the county roads—a palette of reds, yellows and oranges the likes of which have to be seen to be fully appreciated. So, as we talked and got to know one another while driving to our evening hunting grounds, my face was pressed to the glass more often than turned toward Dolen. It was a little rude, perhaps, but forgivable I hope, given the natural distraction competing for my attention.

Eventually, after reaching the end of a gravel road providing access to both an oil well and a grain field, we parked and prepared our gear. To our south was a heavily treed creek valley, while to our north and east lay a series of agricultural fields separated by fences and natural treelines. With a slight breeze from the southeast, the conditions were ideal for hunting our way eastward.

Before setting out, Dolen went over the game plan. We'd walk the field edges, pausing occasionally for him to call, most often mewing like a cow elk and hoping for a response from a randy bull in search of companionship. Periodically, he would also bugle, a no-holds-barred challenge to any resident bull willing to defend his harem from an intruder. The recently harvested field we edged along had been sown with peas, and given the abundance of scat accumulated along the game trail that skirted it, numerous black bears were feasting on the leftovers—more evidence of the region's diverse game.

After walking and intermittently calling for a couple of kilometres, we opted to sit in a 50-metre-wide finger of bush that separated two fields and began to call in earnest.

Bull elk in the Saddle Hills are not especially large when compared with those in the southern foothills. In these parts, a 300-inch bull is pretty good. But what they may lack in size, they more than make up for in numbers. Populations are large and growing, thanks in no small measure to the combination of quality cover and plentiful feed. So every time you call, there's a legitimate expectation of a response.

Game, even as large as elk, have a way of suddenly materializing from out of the trees. One second a field is empty, and the next there's an elk standing in it. And that's just what happened to us, but in our case, there were four elk—a cow, two calves and a bull. Even though they were 800 metres away, from our vantage point, the bull appeared to be worthy of closer inspection.

We made several attempts to call him across the open field with a succession of cow calls and some occasional bugles, but he was having none of it. At one point, the bull exhibited traditional wallowing behaviour, pawing the dirt at his feet, urinating into it, then lying down and rolling around on his back. It was clear that his cow was prime for breeding and wasn't about to abandon her—a bird in the hand, I suppose.

We watched the elk for a full 20 minutes before they slowly walked back east and out of view. Immediately, we were on the move, hugging the treeline for cover as we took the long way around the field to where we'd last seen the elk before they moved off. After a full half-hour, we reached our target destination, a corner with thick brush to the south and east, and open fields to the north and west. Protected by the cover of the trees, we soon found them, about 400 metres due north in another pea field.

The shot angle and distance were more than I was comfortable with, so Dolen began to cow call. The two calves responded immediately. Running straight toward our hiding spot, they closed to within 50 metres as they searched for the cow they were certain they'd heard. At one point, we were sure they had us pinned. With the wind in our favour, however, we were able to outwait them, and soon they wandered off, apparently having lost interest.

For reasons we couldn't fully discern—who knows what goes through the mind of a bull elk—the bull unexpectedly deserted his cow and followed the calves, albeit well behind them. He soon closed to within 150 metres of our lair, and although I couldn't see him, Dolen could, so he elected to cow call in hopes the bull would move into my line of sight. Instead of responding favourably, however, the bull held up, clearly nervous.

At this point, I had no choice but to move or we'd risk the agitated bull clearing out. Reluctantly giving up my spot, I manoeuvred to the other side of Dolen so I could see the bull, now at about 120 metres. I didn't wait. My offhand shot took him through both shoulders, but it took another round before the tough 5x5 would go down. It was 8:00 PM with a half-hour of legal light still ahead of us. I'd been hunting Saddle Hills County for all of about an hour and a half.

Sometimes, it all comes together as though it had been planned exactly that way. Dolen called in to camp for reinforcements, then we began the task of field dressing the bull. Although he was a 5x5, we estimated he was just two and a half years old. He was in beautiful condition, fat and healthy, and the meat would be absolutely wonderful on the dinner plate.

By the time Dolen and I finished prepping him, Mike and the crew from camp had arrived. They were able to drive across the open fields right to where the bull lay, so loading him up was about as easy as it gets in elk country.

Back at camp there were backslaps all around. Another one of the hunters had also tagged a bull, so we hung them side by side to cool in the night air before retiring to the lodge for a nightcap. While I didn't feel the least bit cheated, the drive home would be four times longer than my hunt had lasted, so I wasn't particularly interested in heading home at first light. Fortunately, Dolen invited me to accompany him on a bow hunt the next morning. I gladly accepted because it was far too soon to leave this game-rich area.

So, shortly after first light, Dolen and I found ourselves between those two mature bulls, each screaming their dominance while our calls teased them toward a confrontation. Yes, the hunt eventually went sideways, but I don't think either of us was particularly disappointed. Rutting elk at close quarters represent the apex of the big-game hunting experience, and you would rather repeat it than end it quickly. Besides, Dolen would surely get more opportunities before the season was finished.

As for me? I can only hope that I'll be back in the Saddle again someday soon.

—ɯ—

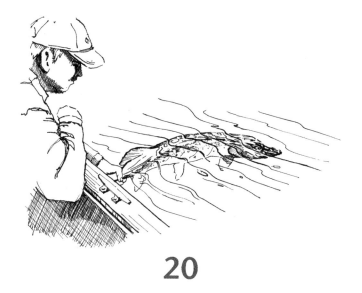

20

ONTARIO MUSKIE MISSION

Some people ask why we catch and release when fishing. They must be the kind of people who don't know the bond we feel when on the water, not just with the fish we catch, but with all of nature and with those with whom we share our fishing experiences. The means are greater than the end. And few fishing experiences demand we catch and release more so than when fishing muskies. You only have to hold a mature muskie in your hands once to know that these are special fish. Further, they're inherent loners, which in some indescribable way only strengthens the bond you forge with them.

I started fishing when I was 9 or 10 years old on southern Ontario's Moira River, and quickly became completely enthralled with anything angling related. What grabbed my attention more than anything else were the mounts of gargantuan muskies hanging in the sporting goods stores, gas stations, barber shops and anywhere else men were likely to gather. Those fish were so big that many were head-mounted, much like you'd see a deer or moose. I suppose this was more affordable and took up considerably less wall space than a full-body mount, but with their toothy mouths agape, these fish heads looked especially menacing to a youngster like me. So, while I continued to dangle my bobber and worm over the local docks for panfish, I vowed that one day I would fight and land a giant muskie of my very own.

Life has a way of making a bird's nest of your plans; however, and our family moved west before my dream could be realized. Over the ensuing years I thought about muskies often, but the opportunity to fish them never came along. Until one October morning I was sitting with a couple friends in my Jon boat over a spread of hand-carved blocks, waiting for the next flight of bluebills to arrive.

One of my duck-hunting companions that morning was Dave Kay, who'd been vacationing at the same resort in northwestern Ontario for 13 years. A wildlife biologist by profession, from year one, Dave set about learning everything he could about muskies and muskie angling, turning his desire and passion into a living laboratory experiment on the cold, clear lake. In those first few seasons, he followed all the conventional muskie best practices, and after three years had accumulated an enviable collection of rods, reels and lures. What he hadn't collected, however, was an honest-to-goodness muskie. But in year four, as his knowledge of the lake and of muskie hunting grew, he boated four. Since then his track record has steadily improved, and over the last couple summers Dave had averaged a muskie of 40 inches or larger every three and a half hours on the water. As we waited patiently in my duck boat, his tales of huge muskies won and lost kept us enthralled

Listening to Dave talk muskies rekindled my desire to catch one. I suppose I could have been coy about it and subtly intimated I'd love to join him. But the Lord hates a coward, and I figured there was little sense in being shy around friends, so I simply invited myself to tag along for a few days. And our other duck-hunting companion that morning, long-time pal Brian Hagglund, figuring it just wouldn't be the same without him, announced he was also available to join in on the fun.

And so it was that Brian and I joined Dave for three days of muskie fishing, to experience firsthand what it's like to hunt, hook and fight Canada's freshwater apex predator. We didn't leave disappointed.

Within the angling community, muskies are referred to with equal parts reverence and disdain as "the fish of 10,000 casts." Those who fish them regularly seem to take some kind of masochistic pride in not being able to catch many of them; withstanding the greatest number of hours while failing to catch a fish appears to earn you a fishing badge of honour. I don't really understand that mentality, and more importantly, neither does Dave. Over the years, Dave has applied his scientific training into understanding the lake he fishes and muskie behaviour there. Through a series of trial and error experiments with tackle and technique, he has refined how to maximize his muskie hunting success. Brian and I were more than willing to take a shortcut to our first muskies by taking advantage of what Dave spent years learning.

We arrived at Randy Hanson's Hideaway Lodge near Lake of the Woods after a three-hour drive from Winnipeg, late on a warm August afternoon. I'd stayed at that lodge more than a decade earlier when Dave and I enjoyed four October days of fishing and hunting. Dave's been returning with his family each summer ever since.

After getting checked in to our little cabin and grabbing a quick bite, Brian and I found Dave down at the dock in his boat, preparing his tackle for the evening fish. After years of experimenting, Dave is convinced that early morning and late evening are the best times for tracking down muskies. We also learned that Dave's strategy is to troll almost exclusively. He followed the conventional muskie playbook for the first several years, casting to humps, reefs and other structure using oversized bucktail spinners with cool names like "Musky Killer" and "Double Cowgirl" before evidence revealed that trolling crankbaits produced more hits than any other tactic.

I really didn't have any expectations that first evening, other than to catch up with old friends while puttering along the broken shoreline of a gorgeous Canadian Shield lake. That would make for a completely satisfying evening in its own right. So I was somewhat surprised when Brian's bouncing rod announced the first fish of the evening. Excited to see a muskie in hand, I cheered Brian on as he began to winch in the fish. It wasn't long into the battle before Dave advised that it wasn't a muskie at the end of the line rather a pike, the muskie's closest cousin. That difference explained why it came in as tame and respectful as an accountant; despite it being a solid 10-pound fish, it was no match for the heavy tackle we were using.

It was nearing pitch dark when Dave's rod went off. He immediately proclaimed it as a muskie, and we went into a pitcrew–like fury with me jumping to the helm while Brian prepared the net. Unfortunately, it all served as little more than practice because only a minute into the fight, Dave's line when slack. Somehow the great fish had become unstuck. Undaunted, we were only marginally disappointed as we motored back to camp. We'd had a wonderful evening catching up with one another, and the action we experienced was mere icing on the cake. There would be better days ahead.

The next morning broke sunny and clear with a slight breeze, ideal fishing conditions. We were on the water by 7:30 AM, Dave at the helm with his eyes glued to the lake map he had created over the years that carefully marks the location of every muskie he's hooked. That map had become his bible, and it seemed to me that if he examined it any more closely, out of respect he'd need to start wearing rubber gloves. After weighing history and all the influencing variables of the day, Dave chose our starting position. When we got to the section of shoreline he'd selected, we rigged up the massive crankbaits that have proven themselves on the lake, tossed them 25 metres behind the boat then settled in to troll. I was pulling a large lure called a Bucher Depth Raider; the cool name alone gave me confidence.

When you've been trolling for hours without so much as a bump, it's easy to fall into a landscape-infused stupor. The ceaseless gurgle of the motor and the whisper of the wind on a warm and sunny August morning are more effective at putting you into a near-trance than Reveen could be on his best day. So I nearly jumped out of my skin when the portside rod jerked violently in the holder, signalling a fish. Instantly awake and alert, I fought with the rod to get it out of the holder, cursing the fact that they are never as easy to extract as they are to insert. With the rod eventually in hand, I wrestled it into some level of control against the heavy pull that threatened to separate me from the gear. Eventually, I assumed command, and for a fleeting moment, was aware that if I didn't make a mistake in the subsequent several minutes—if the fish didn't throw the hook or straighten it out, if it wasn't accidentally knocked free during the landing process and if the fishing gods didn't simply decide I wasn't yet deserving—my near 50-year desire to land a muskie would soon come to a rewarding conclusion.

Uninitiated anglers believe that a muskie is not much different than a pike, unless it happens to be a really big muskie. Well, I've fished pike for 40 years, and it became immediately clear to me that this was no pike. Whatever was on the end of my line had immense strength and would peel line whenever it felt the urge. Even with my drag turned way down, I'd gain a little line then immediately lose it. That this was no pike was a little like saying that Oedipus was a mama's boy; there was no doubt whatsoever. After a furious game of tug of war, I eventually brought it to the net then lifted it out for the obligatory photos and a quick measurement. The fish stretched the tape to just over 38 inches but was fat, thick and deep. I gently released it, watching it swim back to its frigid lair before whooping with excitement. My first muskie was now but a memory.

After backslaps all around, we settled back to the game, tossing out our lures and resuming our trolling run. As we moved into slightly deeper water, I switched up to a Shad Rap in natural perch colours. It was less than an hour later that my rod bounced again, and before I knew it was into my second fish. Although it turned out to be a couple inches longer than the first, this one came in a little easier. Until it saw the boat, that is, whereupon it began thrashing violently, as though it's very life depended upon it. After some give and take, it settled down sufficiently for Brian to slide the net under it. While *we* assumed the battle was over, the muskie had other thoughts. It had taken the hook deeply, and realizing we risked damaging it trying to remove the hook, Dave used his wire cutters to snip the offending barb. Once the line and lure were free, I reached into the net to hold the massive fish aloft.

I knew immediately that something was wrong. A pain worse than a horseradish enema consumed me. I figured that as I'd slid my hand under the gill plate to control the struggling muskie, I'd somehow impaled my thumb on one or more of its fearsome teeth. I called to Dave to take the weight of the fish from me, and as he did so, I realized that I'd stuck myself with the hook that was still lodged firmly in its maw. Free of the fish's weight, and with a little wiggling, I was able to free my thumb. After quick photo session, I slipped the muskie back into the lake with a derisive slap of its tail telling us it was healthy and glad to be rid of us. Meanwhile, a trail of blood seeping from my now tender thumb followed me around the boat, a crimson reminder that muskies are powerful fish and vigilance is required when handling them. I grabbed a towel to staunch the flow, but it was a full week before I didn't feel a painful reminder of that fish every time I bumped my ragged thumb.

With two fish landed, we were a happy boat, although the rest of the morning was uneventful. Still, two mature muskies within an hour demonstrated just how precise Dave had become in understanding how, when and where to target them on this lake.

We went out again that evening, fishing from 7:00 until 11:30 PM, well past the time that the veil of darkness descended on the lake. Motoring home in the black was a little like playing dodgeball; we were never sure exactly which way to turn to avoid the many reefs and sunken humps that pepper the lake. Dave's years of experience on the lake revealed itself to be a blessing in a newfound way. I'm positive I could never have navigated our way back to the dock in the dark without an ugly incident.

The following morning we were back on the lake at 6:30, our confidence buoyed by the previous day's success. But five hours later, we hit the dock without getting so much as a nibble, save for a lone smallmouth bass that committed hari-kari on Brian's lure that was nearly as big as the bass itself. Our results were similar that evening despite fishing for another four hours.

Dave, somewhat discouraged and feeling a little unwarranted pressure, said that it was unusual for him to fish an entire day without hooking into at least one muskie. So, in the time-tested manner of fishermen worldwide, we proceeded to try to explain the unexplainable, offering suggestions ranging from air pressure and water temperature to the moon phase in trying to rationalize our lack of success. At the end of the day, however, we simply needed to remind ourselves that muskies are lone, pelagic predators that live by their own whims and haven't earned the "fish of 10,000 casts" moniker by accident.

Our final day on the water began much the same as the previous one. We fished all morning without a single strike. But we had one more evening to fish, and as experienced sportsmen, we knew that in the immortal words of Yogi Berra, "It ain't over 'til it's over." So Brian and I went back to our cabin for lunch and our midday snooze still optimistic that we weren't done as muskie hunters just yet. As I settled onto the couch, a little guilt kept me from fully relaxing. I had two fish in the boat while Brian hadn't hooked up yet. Having fished for as long as I have, I know that's it's often just a matter of luck when two or more anglers are doing exactly the same thing but one is tagging up while the other isn't. It happens. Still, when it's a fish as elusive and hard won as a muskie, I really wanted Brian to experience the excitement that I had.

I guess I must have dozed off eventually, because I jolted up in shock when I heard Dave's voice through the window screen.

"Get up, guys. The weather's turning, and we need to get out on the lake. Now!"

Dave isn't the kind of guy to waste words. He's one of those guys with all of the vices I admire and none of the virtues I detest, to borrow from Churchill. So when he says it's time to go, it's time to go. Brian and I stumbled out from our semi-slumber into mid-afternoon gun-metal grey skies, scudding clouds and increasing winds.

"The bite's usually on leading up to a storm," Dave advised, "and we need to get onto the water before it gets nasty."

So out we went, Dave running the boat at top speed to the cluster of islands he wanted us to fish. We could see, feel and taste the weather worsening as we hurried to get the gear in the water.

Twenty minutes in, Brian's rod went off. It was a bit more of a rodeo than usual given the wind and waves, and Dave was busy at the helm keeping us off the rocks while I cleared space in the boat and readied the net, praying I wouldn't do something stupid like knock the fish off the hook in the landing process. As Dave and I dutifully did our jobs, Brian bore down on what was clearly a good fish, and after a 10-minute tussle brought it to the boat and into the waiting net. Everybody had done their job to perfection. As the boat bounced and rolled in the growing swells, we captured some photos then released the big hen. At a shade over 42 inches, it was the largest muskie of the trip.

Looking up after returning the big muskie to her home, the closing weather made it clear it was also time for us to head for home. Thunder cracked, lightening flashed and the skies opened up as we steered for camp. We were soon soaked to the skin. But despite our rain-drenched faces, our smiles lit up the dock as we landed safely.

By the end of the three days, we had landed three mature muskies, the longest stretching the tape to 42 inches, a complete success by nearly any measure. The fishing may have been slow by Dave's standards, but as far as we could tell, no other boats on the lake landed so much as a single fish.

On pressured lakes, muskies can become conditioned, so it often pays to try something different from what other anglers are doing.

Although Dave had become accustomed to trolling this lake's steep breaks because it works, he also planned to also troll the kilometre-long flats in five to eight metres of water. They're the places Dave jigs for bass with his family through the midday hours, but he believes they could also be ideal, unpressured feeding grounds for muskies under the cover of darkness. Such dedication to trial and error is what has transformed him from a muskie wannabe into a muskie master. As for his plan to troll for muskies on the flats after dark? I have absolutely no idea if it's a good strategy or not, but I aim to be in the boat alongside him when he finds out.

—m—

21

IN THE LAND OF LIVING SKIES

I'm admittedly biased about my home province of Alberta, especially when it comes to angling and hunting opportunities. If you enjoy a broad spectrum of fish, game and landscapes, you'd be hard-pressed to find greater diversity than we have. That doesn't mean, however, that for some individual species, or suites of related species, that other provinces or regions don't offer greater abundance and opportunity. And so it is with waterfowl that take advantage of agricultural crops each fall. I'm referring specifically to Canada, white-fronted and snow geese, along with mallards, pintails and the strange and ancient sandhill crane. These are at or near the top of the most desired waterfowl across Canada, and if you want reliable, consistent hunting for these species, it's tough to beat the Saskatchewan experience.

The residents of Saskatchewan were more prophetic than they imagined when selecting "The Land of Living Skies" as the slogan for their license plates. Undoubtedly referring to the border-to-border vistas dominated by the seemingly endless azure skies they enjoy, their motto could just as easily allude to the millions of waterfowl that trade on the province's prairie winds every year. Saskatchewan constitutes the heart of North America's renowned Prairie Pothole Region, the epicentre of our continent's waterfowl breeding habitat. Also celebrated for its grain production, a favourite food of migrating ducks and geese, given that the whole of Saskatchewan is home to barely more than a million people, it's little wonder that waterfowling hotspots abound throughout the province. And while many of these areas have deservedly earned international acclaim as waterfowling destinations, I've fallen hard for the southeastern region, where staggering numbers of geese, ducks and sandhill cranes make for a spectacular trifecta of bird-hunting opportunities. Living skies indeed.

I was first introduced to southeastern Saskatchewan some 25 years ago. An old friend and I met in Yorkton, he travelling west from Winnipeg while I headed down from Edmonton—it seemed like a practical meeting point for getting together to hunt geese and spend a few days catching up. In the afternoons and evenings we'd scout for feeding birds and secure permission to hunt. Not once did we fail to find geese, nor did we have difficulty in getting access permission. The relative lack of hunting pressure coupled with welcoming landowners is one of Saskatchewan's many charms.

This was the era of goose chairs—oversized Canada goose decoys affixed to a reclined soccer mom chair of sorts.

In the mornings we'd put out our spread—three dozen G&H Canada goose shells and another two or three dozen silhouette duck decoys. The silhouettes were made from half-inch plywood cut roughly in the shape of a "head-up" mallard, then spray-painted matte black (barbecue paint was our enamel of choice for the task). We'd face our goose chairs downwind surrounded by a shallow u-shaped spread of decoys, our layout limited in size and density by the few decoys we had to work with. By today's standards, the set-up was small and rudimentary. Nonetheless, on three consecutive mornings we enjoyed tremendous shoots of Canada geese and ducks, an equal mix of pintails and mallards. We didn't limit out on each hunt, which was more a function of our shooting prowess than opportunity. But it was just that quickly that I became a convert; I vowed this would not be the last time I would hunt the region.

Time has a way of conspiring against our recreational aspirations. It would be almost 10 years before I'd get back, this time lured by the prospect of sandhill cranes, a species I'd never previously hunted. A work friend had hunted cranes in Saskatchewan for many years and invited me to experience for myself what all the growing crane fuss was about. Home base would be the town of Wynyard on the southeast corner of the renowned Quill Lakes, one of the most widely recognized waterfowl staging wetlands in prairie Canada and a Mecca for dedicated waterfowlers. Wynyard is a small, hunter-friendly town just 140 kilometres northwest of Yorkton. In those days the motels and restaurants all posted signs welcoming hunters, even amending their schedules and amenities to accommodate the typical "working hours" of visiting hunters.

I soon learned that hunting cranes is not a lot different than hunting geese. Spotting is 75 percent of the battle, and sandhills, like Canadas, love their grain fields for fine dining. Another constant is the general disdain farmers have for cranes, geese and ducks alike when the birds are wreaking havoc on uncombined swaths, contributing to the ever-present welcome mat afforded hunters in these parts.

We headed southeast from Wynyard, down the high-way towards Foam Lake, another typical rural Saskatchewan community that is the namesake of a lake just a handful of kilometres northwest. On reflection, it may be the lake that's the namesake; I really don't know. In either case, Foam Lake (the lake, that is) has a reputation for being an important local roost for cranes. We were still a good 10 kilometres from the lake when we saw the first skeins of sandhills sifting westward. As when planning to hunt any waterfowl in the field, once you've got birds off the roost and into the air, the strategy is to pursue them in hopes of pinpointing where they're feeding. Over the course of the late afternoon and early evening, we followed wave after wave of cranes as they headed out to feed. We soon had several likely fields identified.

As a crane-hunting neophyte, I didn't really question why we had neither blinds nor decoys with us. My partner seemed to know what he was doing, and I was content to sit back, observe and soak in as much knowledge as I could. This was my opportunity to learn the tricks of the trade from a crane guru, and I wasn't about to question anything, no matter how strange it seemed to me. Besides, travelling light is always preferable to hauling a ton of gear around. Provided your success isn't compromised, of course.

As I was to learn, there are two broadly accepted yet widely dissimilar tactics for hunting sandhill cranes. There are those who hunt them much like they hunt geese, setting up blinds and decoys in feeding fields. When all goes right you're shooting cranes at relatively close range as they settle into your spread. The alternative approach is to pass shoot them. Now, pass shooting is considered by some to be the lazy man's approach to waterfowling. Requiring minimal equipment, in essence, it's all about intercepting birds as they fly from one location to another. As a rule it's not a particularly effective tactic for geese and ducks, although most hunters have done it at one time or another. It typically means long shots, and given that most pass shooting takes place from headlands or roadside rights-of-way on public land, retrieval of downed birds can be a challenge.

Cranes, it turns out, are an altogether different kettle of fish, or birds as it were. They're much more predictable in their flight path from roost to feeding field than are ducks or geese, as though they follow lane markers in the sky. They also tend to fly relatively low when heading out to feed, meaning shots are not as long. Ironically, for birds that appear somewhat ungainly and prehistoric on land, they're both refined and graceful on the wing.

Those first crane hunts were a resounding success. With no decoys or blinds, we were clearly there with the intention of pass shooting. Positioned along grassy fence lines or behind round bales, we shot near limits on two consecutive mornings. Most often the cranes would fly on precisely the same path they had when we'd spotted them the previous evening, though on occasion we had to sprint down the fence line or between bales to better position ourselves for the next flight. Most importantly, over those two days, I learned just how much fun crane hunting can be.

Sandhill cranes get a bad rap from many hunters and are commonly referred to as "lawn darts" or "pterodactyls" because of their unusual appearance. They are also called "ninjas" because if they come down wounded, they'll stand with bill poised to strike any man or dog that approaches. The pose can be quite intimidating, and they're both willing and capable of backing up the threat. Dogs, in particular, must be careful when retrieving wounded cranes. All legs and bills, they are unbelievably noisy when circling decoys, but those unique physical characteristics introduce an undeniably entertaining element to the hunt. It's been said that when a crane is shot from the sky, it comes down like a broken lawn chair, a description I find to be remarkably accurate.

Another common belief among those who don't hunt cranes is that they're not very good to eat. I came away from my first crane experience having completely erased that idea, and to this day I prefer a young crane on the table to any Canada goose. In fact, those in the know often refer to cranes as "the ribeye of the sky.".

It would be a few more years before I would again experience the abundance of opportunity that southeast Saskatchewan offers waterfowlers. Fortunately, at the invitation of a couple of hunting product manufacturers, for two consecutive falls I had the pleasure of hunting from Tony Vandemore's renowned Habitat Flats camp, located just outside Yorkton. Tony's is a first-class outfitter, from ultra-comfortable camp facilities and home-cooked meals to professional guides using the latest in equipment. At Tony's camp, we hunted from the latest A-frame blinds; comfortable, roomy enough, and when fully dressed with natural vegetation, they look amazingly natural, especially when backed against a slough margin or native shrubs. They're certainly a far cry from sitting in goose chairs or cowering behind a hay bale! As to decoys, we had more goose and duck blocks than I cared to count. And when hunting cranes, several dozen full-bodied decoys did the trick, each painted so realistically that you have to get pretty close to distinguish them from the real thing.

My first time at Tony's camp I hunted with the folks from SportDOG, a company that makes electronic collars for hunting dogs. There were four or five writers along with four or five representatives from SportDOG, plus a guide or two, and the plan was that everybody would hunt together. The prospect of effectively hiding a dozen people was no small task, but Tony and his crew were up to the challenge, assisted in no small part by the huge numbers of birds in the area and relatively few other hunters. A typical day saw us shoot cranes in the morning and ducks in the afternoon. Over two days we took 80 cranes, several dozen mallards and a handful of Canada geese. By the time I started my nine-hour drive home, I'd been clearly reminded why this region of Saskatchewan is revered in waterfowling circles across the continent.

The next fall I was invited back to Habitat Flats to join Dennis and Doug Brune, the owners of ALPS Outdoorz, a company that makes a wide variety of quality outdoor gear, including many products designed specifically for waterfowl hunters. They're both gentlemen of the highest order, and it was easy to enjoy their company. Joining us was Skip Knowles, the editor of *Wildfowl* magazine. I'd hunted previously with Skip and knew him to be worth the price of admission every time. He's one of those guys who blends a healthy cynicism, a wry sense of humour and a deep passion for waterfowl hunting. The combination can be pretty comical or a little intimidating depending upon his mood, but I always get a kick out of him.

If you think about hunting flooded timber, undoubtedly Arkansas or Mississippi come to mind; certainly not Saskatchewan. But there'd been considerable rainfall that summer and fall, and on our first afternoon, we found ourselves knee-deep in water flooding out a small copse of trees. The ducks were piling in to drink before jumping out to feed in a nearby field. A dozen floating decoys offered them all the encouragement they needed, and we blazed away as though we were deep in Confederate country. Skip even knocked down a wayward goose that flew over to see what all the fuss was about. I've come to expect world-class waterfowl hunting when I visit this part of Saskatchewan, but a flooded timber hunt tops the cake!

Our next day was more typical with a crane hunt in the morning and an afternoon mallard shoot. Under an overcast sky, we had cyclones of ducks spinning around our decoys, predominantly mallards, but strangely enough, good numbers of green-winged teal as well. I'm still not certain why they were there, but we didn't argue, actively selecting for the tasty little ducks.

The last morning's duck hunt was more typical, although we did have a surprising visitor show up late to the party. There were 20 mallards and a pintail drake piled up behind the blind, and we were thinking about packing up when a lone drake wood duck, resplendent in breeding plumage, buzzed through the blocks. If there's a prettier duck than a fully plumed wood duck, I've not seen it. After it tumbled to the ground in front of the blind, Brad, our guide, asked if he could take the bird to have it mounted. Considering that at least three of us had shot simultaneously when that woodie cruised into range, none of us could claim ownership of the bird. Letting Brad take it home seemed like a fitting option.

From many perspectives, my experiences those two falls were a significant departure from my earlier forays to the region. In part that reflects the passing of time and the associated evolution of hunting gear; it also speaks to the difference between do-it-yourself hunting and being pampered by professionals. Yet despite these differences, one thing hadn't changed a lick over 25-plus years; southeast Saskatchewan remains a near unparalleled destination for waterfowlers.

The birds have changed a little over the years but all for the better. Pintail numbers have recovered meaningfully since their record lows of the mid '90s, and mallard numbers have absolutely sky-rocketed since then. Canada geese continue to be abundant, and unprecedented upturns in continental snow goose populations have provided increased options in the fall and an altogether new hunting opportunity in the spring. As for sandhill cranes, enormous flocks of our oldest surviving bird species continues to trace those living skies every fall. The good old days of waterfowling? In southeast Saskatchewan, we're living them.

—꿈—

22

TOMFOOLERY

Outdoor Canada has the largest circulation of any outdoors publication in the country, and I'm fortunate to have been a columnist and regular contributor there for the past 25 years. Despite the complexities of publishing a magazine, the team that puts it together is pretty small. Patrick Walsh has been my editor since 2000, and he leads a crew of two assistant editors and a designer, as well as a small team of advertising sales-people. Tim McEachern led that team for several years. Despite me living three provinces away from head office, we're a pretty tight-knit group. We see each other at annual trade shows but seldom beyond that, so having the opportunity to share time afield with them only strengthens our bond. Besides that, they're just damn fun people to be around.

As the pilot's voice crackles over the intercom announcing we're about to begin our descent into Toronto, I pause from reading my book and ask myself just what the heck I'm doing. The cost of airfare alone should have made me think twice about this, let alone all the other associated costs, from licenses and shells to food and more. All to chase a turkey. If everything went well I'd return five days later with about five pounds of wild turkey meat and a few turkey trinkets, including a beard and a tail feather. I couldn't help myself from doing the math; rough calculations put it at about $200 per pound, more costly than the best Kobe beef.

But as with all hunting, the return on investment isn't based on food value. I wasn't seeking wild turkey meat in particular, as scrumptious as that is; I was laying my hard-earned cash on the table in return for an experience. Because I'd discovered in my three previous hunts with Tim McEachern and Patrick Walsh that chasing turkeys is a highly addictive pursuit.

I'm not the only one who has succumbed to the turkey's charms; in the U.S., turkeys rank second in popularity among hunters only to the ubiquitous white-tailed deer. For many years, I didn't understand what all the fuss was about. Then I got hooked and look forward to my annual trip as much or more than I do any other single hunt.

What makes turkey hunting so compelling is difficult to put your finger on. It's not that you're going to fill your freezer. And it's certainly not that they're a particularly beautiful bird, as some might describe a full-plumage mallard or pheasant. In fact, by most standards turkeys are odd-looking, if not downright unattractive. I suppose it boils down to a combination of their other-worldly senses and their "street smarts," attributes that are difficult to quantify or chronicle.

Legend has it that no less an insightful thinker than Benjamin Franklin, renowned U.S. scientist, inventor, politician, businessman and founding father, is purported to have said that he wished Americans had selected the turkey rather than the bald eagle as their national symbol. This isn't exactly true, and in an era when dispelling fake news is all the rage, perhaps some clarification is in order.

According to my research, the origins of the myth arise in a letter Franklin sent to his daughter, apparently referencing the seal of the Society of Cincinnati, a club that to this day celebrates the successes of the Revolutionary War. (By the way, the society took its name from Lucius Quinctius Cincinnatus, a hero of the Roman Republic, not from the Ohio city.) The society had chosen an eagle for their seal, and Franklin supposedly was making a joke that denigrated the image, suggesting the eagle on the seal looked more like a turkey.

According to Franklin biographers, in that letter to his daughter Franklin wrote, "For my own part I wish the Bald Eagle had not been chosen...He is a Bird of bad moral Character. He does not get his Living honestly." As for the turkey, Franklin went on to write that it "was a much more respectable bird...and a bird of courage."

The Franklin legend aside, "respectable" only begins to describe a wild turkey. More often they're described as "smart," "wily" or something similar. Despite their rather unusual appearance that contributes to the impression by some that these must be dull-witted creatures, it takes considerable skill to outsmart what is surely one of our sharpest game animals. Consider that from the time it has hatched, a wild turkey is a target for predators. As a result, he's equipped with unique defenses to stymie his foes, including the two-legged, camouflage-clad variety. His powerful legs allow him to sprint at 40 kilometres per hour, and his telescopic eyesight has a 270-degree field of view. Give a turkey the chance, and he'll see a hunter blink at 100 metres. He sees what you can't see, and he hears what you can't hear. To make matters even more challenging, turkeys are social creatures and seldom travel alone, so hunters must often contend with multiple sets of these incredible eyes and ears.

With a loud thump that left me momentarily wondering if we'd landed or been shot down, we hit the runway and I emerged from my thoughts, refocusing on the days ahead. If they were to be anything like my previous Ontario turkey hunts, I was in for four days of camaraderie, lots of laughs, no shortage of surprises, and just maybe, a turkey in the bag.

Tim and Patrick were both experienced turkey hunters when they first invited me to join them. My turkey hunting history, on the other hand, was limited to two days in Alberta, which represented all the time I could free up the one year I was drawn for a tag. I had two takeaways from that first experience. First, hunting turkeys wasn't quite the "fish in a barrel" proposition I'd imagined it might be. And second, given it now takes about 15 years to draw a tag, my Alberta turkey hunting days were likely over. So I was appreciative when the invite from Tim and Patrick arrived.

Headquarters for our hunt would be Tim's hunting camp, a tidy bungalow in the small community of Riversdale, south of the Bruce Peninsula. Prior to my invite I'd never heard of Riversdale, and I suspect that you could live within 160 kilometres of the place and never have heard of it. It's small, little more than a loose collection of a couple dozen houses. The boundary between where the community ends and the agricultural landscape begins is blurred beyond recognition. But as I've come to discover, what it may lack in size, it more than makes up for in charm.

As a youth Tim had a friend whose parents owned a place in Riversdale, and for many years hunted and fished in the area. He eventually bought his own place there, hunting turkeys each spring, and deer and waterfowl during the fall months. After 50 years hunting the region, he knows the landscape, and more importantly, the landowners pretty well.

I got to know Tim when he was the advertising sales manager for *Outdoor Canada* magazine, where I've been a long-time contributor. Patrick Walsh has been editor of the publication for nearly 20 years. Suffice to say, the three of us knew one another pretty well, though we'd never hunted together.

For most of that first season, I kept my mouth closed and my eyes and ears open. Tim has taken more turkeys over the years than he can count, so I knew that if I played my cards right, I would learn a whole lot about gobblers in a short time. I sat where he told me to sit, called when and how he told me to call and even dressed how he suggested I should dress. I was the student, and he was the mentor, a name that's stuck with him in our little group throughout the intervening years.

On our second morning, the three of us were hunting together, concealed in the treeline alongside a crop field just beginning to emerge. Tim was sitting near enough to me that we could communicate in hushed tones, while Patrick was hunkered down about 50 metres away. I was learning the language of turkeys as the boys took turns making sounds imitating a hen seeking companionship. When I heard that first gobble, the hairs on the back of my neck stood up. It was a spooky moment. I mean, I knew what to expect if a tom was in the vicinity, but hearing that first one answer our calls was exhilarating.

Everything got dead serious at that point. We ceased all unnecessary movement, and my senses came to full alert. The tone of Tim's calling took on a more urgent tone. Ten minutes into the back and forth between Tim and the gobbler, the increased volume of the tom told me he was closing the distance. Minutes later I saw movement in my peripheral vision and turned my head ever so slowly. There he was in full strut, tail fanned, featherless head ablaze in red and blue, slowly working towards our hen decoy 30 metres in front of us.

Later, the boys would ask why I waited so long to shoot. All I know is I'd been reminded more than once not to be impatient, to wait until the turkey was comfortably in range before hitting the switch. That patience mantra rang loud in my mind as the big tom advanced. He seemed confident in what he was doing, and my shotgun was at the ready, balanced comfortably over my knees, so I didn't feel the need to rush. Late to the party as I may have been, when I did finally shoot, the gobbler collapsed where he stood next to the decoy, his wings flapping furiously as he breathed his last. Success! My first wild turkey was in the bag. We hustled out to admire it, all three of us grinning ear to ear. In the end it hadn't been so difficult, and for a moment I considered announcing myself a certified turkey master equal to Tim. Discretion, however, suggested I keep that to myself, which as future events would show was sage advice.

When we reconvened at Tim's camp in year two, I arrived with much more confidence; the lessons I'd absorbed the previous season were still fresh in my mind. I was ready for advanced training, but figured I had the basics down and could hunt a little more independently. Eager with anticipation, we were out of camp that first morning by 5:15, fueled by coffee so strong it could float a 3 ½-inch load of #4s. We began to call at first light and immediately heard gobbling in response. But despite our collective best efforts, it wasn't long before all the toms went quiet. We assumed they must have "henned up" and had no need to chase companionship when they had a willing partner at hand. By 8:00 AM we'd picked up and were headed back for the truck. As luck would have it, not a mile down the trail we spied a tom, a jake and six hens in a fallow field. It would have been pointless trying to call the tom away from his harem, so we discussed the possibility of a stalk. Normally, trying to sneak up on a crafty gobbler is as fruitless as a January apple tree, but the old tom had his hands full wrangling the hens while keeping the upstart jake at bay, and Patrick managed to crawl his way to within the outer edge of practical range. He took the shot but didn't connect, and the birds scuttled hurriedly into cover. That ended up being our only opportunity of the day.

The next morning's hunt was equally futile, so we headed over to a farm we'd hunted the previous year. Dale and Natasha are about as friendly and welcoming as landowners can be. They insist on serving us après-hunt refreshments every time we visit, served over the bar Dale has erected in his machine shed. The shed is more an oversized man cave, decorated with an eclectic mix of sports memorabilia, antiques and various collectibles. The woodstove is always lit, and as we gathered around the warmth of the bar, Dale's bottomless repertoire of stories kept us entertained until we're in danger of having a beer too many. Eventually, one of has to call "time" and shepherd the other two back to the truck.

We have a favourite field we like to hunt at Dale's, and on this afternoon we spread ourselves around its perimeter. It was blowing pretty hard with a steady rain falling, so our expectations weren't high. But we were there to hunt, so we did. I set up a hen decoy about 30 metres in front of where I sat concealed in some brambles and began to work the box call as Tim had taught me.

His lessons must have stuck because, amazingly enough, only 20 minutes after I began my calling sequence, a tom and three hens strode confidently out from cover. I waited patiently for the gobbler to approach the decoy, but something was clearly amiss because he wouldn't fully commit. Eventually, I decided it was now or never and took the 45-metre shot. The old tom never so much as ruffled a feather, collapsing where he stood, stone dead.

My instinct was to immediately rush out and claim my prize, but inexplicably the hens hadn't spooked. I continued to sit, hoping the three live decoys supplementing my plastic imitation would entice out another gobbler. Ten minutes later, however, the hens, for reasons only they know, walked into the bush and out of sight. That provided the opportunity to retrieve my tom, so I got up from my hidey-hole and strode confidently toward the fallen turkey.

The problem with experience is that you usually don't get it until about 10 minutes after you needed it. I was about two-thirds the way to that gobbler when he lifted his head, looked this way and that, then jumped to his feet and took off like he'd been shot out of a cannon. I stood there in amazement, alternately watching the old boy run over a succession of rises in the forest and staring lustfully back to my shotgun, propped neatly against a tree. That tom hadn't moved a muscle in the 10 minutes before I went to fetch him! Note to self: Never leave your shotgun behind when you go out to make a retrieve no matter how convinced you are that your tom has well and truly gone to meet his maker.

Tim admitted later he'd seen this possum-like behaviour once before, but that didn't stop him or Patrick from laughing at my folly for the rest of the day and well into the evening.

I'm nothing if not determined, so the next afternoon we were back at Dale's, and I was reclined in my same little nest with my decoy back at work. Patrick and Tim were hidden in their respective ambush points on other sides of the field; if a turkey slipped from cover anywhere, one of us would see it.

It was about a half-hour later when my cell phone flashed a text message. It was Patrick, reporting that a gobbler had stepped out of the bush about 200 metres to my left, walking parallel to the trees in my direction. I scrunched down a little lower, made sure my gear was well-hidden and got my shotgun into position. The wait was interminable. How long does it take a turkey to walk a couple hundred metres? I knew better than to get impatient and shift my position to sneak a peek. Eventually, my patience paid off, and the tom waltzed into view. He was about 60 metres from where I sat, but if he continued on his path, he'd walk to within 30. I trained my barrel on the perfect spot, ensuring

I had a clear shooting lane through the brush, and waited. When he finally stepped into sight. I took aim on his outstretched neck and carefully squeezed the trigger.

"Click." Click!? What the hell? I worked the slide as rapidly as I could, ramming a fresh round into the chamber. The tom was on the move, and I was forced to take a hurried shot. From his reaction, I could tell I'd hit him though not fatally. Then that old tom did something I thought I'd never see. Rather than continuing to run towards the safety of the trees, which would have ensured his escape, he launched himself skyward. I jumped to my feet, swung my smoothbore much as I would when leading a crossing duck and fired. At the shot, the big gobbler veered straight vertical, reaching about 80 meters before dropping like stone. I could hear the thud from where I stood.

From across the way, I could hear the guys laughing at the sight of my little escapade. Talking later, I'm not sure they believed my story of a misfire, choosing instead to assume I must not have closed the action properly. I had borrowed the shotgun from Tim so I didn't have much familiarity with it, but these aren't exactly complicated devices. I was positive it had been a gun or shell issue. Thankfully, we were to later discover that there had been a piece of woody debris in the action that prevented it from functioning properly.

That evening a number of the locals dropped by Tim's place, as they often do when we're hunting. Most I suspect are just trying to escape the repetition of daily life, since Riversdale isn't exactly a beehive of activity most nights. Cory, a young sheep and grain farmer from just down the road, stopped in, a soft-spoken guy who defines the new era of gentlemen farmers, and invited us to join him, his wife and family for dinner on a subsequent evening. The graciousness of this community never ceases to amaze me. Steve, an electrician who works at the nearby nuclear power station, and a regular visitor to Tim's camp, also came by for a beer, as did Joe, a long-haul trucker with a heart as big as his rig. We regaled them with the tales of our turkey adventures; they, meanwhile, offered scouting reports of turkeys they'd seen going about their daily business.

Heading home that year, I concluded that I actually understood very little about turkey hunting, despite the first-class mentoring I was receiving. Nothing I'd read or heard had prepared me for zombie turkeys rising from the dead or toms that elect to fly rather than run away.

Year three was altogether different. Where we'd seen turkeys previously, spots where Tim finds birds every year, we saw nothing, and got no reaction to our plaintive calling. These turkeys should have been on milk cartons they'd disappeared so suddenly and so completely.

Each day after the morning hunt, we'd stop by a convenience store in the nearby town of Teeswater to pick up milk, bread and whatever supplies we needed. And every morning, right as rain, the Korean proprietor, Tommy Lee, would ask how we made out that morning. Day after day, we had to confess we'd struck out, and Tommy would laugh good-naturedly at our incompetence, usually peppering his laughter with some well-chosen words that reinforced his opinion. This went on for several days and became something of a running joke at our expense.

On the last day, after another quiet morning, we pulled in one last time to Dale's, hoping our luck might change. Much of the afternoon was more of the same, the three of us calling and nobody answering. Tim and I were concealed next to each other so that we could at least visit and commiserate on our last hunt together for the year. Finally, a couple hours into our afternoon, movement to my left caught my attention. There, huddled up against the barbed-wire fence just seven metres away, stood a flock of seven jakes staring out at our decoy. At this point I was more than willing to take a jake, but as a southpaw shooter would have to swing completely around to face them. There was no way they'd hang around through that contortion, so I froze in place, hoping they'd toddle out into the open. Alas, they quickly sensed something wasn't right and disappeared back into the trees as quickly as they'd materialized.

Turkey hunting, like all hunting for that matter, demands that you stay positive until the last vestige of legal light has died. It's about enduring a series of unforeseen mishaps and sticking with it until one of the haps fails to miss. And so it was, late that afternoon that a lone tom, most likely fed up with the constant stream of hen calls reverberating through his living room, decided to investigate. Textbook perfect, he waddled along the bush line, through the trees and eventually straight up to our decoy. I couldn't have missed if I'd tried.

After picking up, we headed straight to Tommy Lee's convenience store. I hefted the big tom over my shoulder, pushed through the door and smugly plopped the still warm bird on the counter right next to the register. With the three of us giggling like school girls and Tommy loudly protesting in his thick accent, "He's too beeeg; he's too beeeg," we made quite a spectacle for the dumbfounded customers in his store.

As I waited at the airport for Patrick to pick me up and drive to camp for our fourth season together, I smiled with anticipation. I didn't know what sort of tomfoolery awaited us this year, but I couldn't wait to find out.

—៣—

AND BEYOND...

While the theme of this book is angling and hunting across Canada, following are two adventures from beyond our borders. I've included them in this compilation because each has a distinct link to Canada. The first is a tale of hunting and fishing in Greenland and Iceland. Greenland is closer to Canada in terms of distance, landforms and wildlife than it is to any other country. Our geography and history are closely linked, and if you enjoy Canada's Arctic, you'll recognize and love Greenland. Or at least the part of it that's accessible.

The second story takes place in Namibia, about as far away from Canada as you can get, not only when measured in air miles, but also in terms of its ecology and history. The link, in this case, relates to my pursuit of a Macnab, a fishing and hunting challenge whose roots originate in a 1925 novel written by John Buchan, a Scottish novelist and politician who died in office while serving as Canada's 15th Governor General.

23

WHERE VIKINGS ROAMED

The weather was deteriorating as we boated from Greenland's Narsarsuaq Airport to the caribou camp on Imartuneq Bay, but the drizzle did little to hide the vast landscape's natural beauty. From a distance, the verdant shores appeared muted as if hiding behind a watercolour wash, but whenever we neared the steep cliffs, a multitude of vibrant green hues emerged. Around us, the foamy sea was pockmarked with white and deep cerulean blue icebergs, some small and posing little threat while others loomed like frozen skyscrapers. Despite the gusting winds, I stood outside the shelter of the boat's cabin, awestruck by the sheer magnitude of the stark and colourful vista.

Perched on the rocky shores at the end of a protected bay, the camp that would be home for the next several days soon came into sight. It was reminiscent of most remote Arctic outposts I've visited; a dozen wooden cabins formed a semicircle around the main lodge, each cabin featuring two beds, electric lighting and an electric heater. Washroom facilities, including hot showers and a sauna (this was Greenland after all!), were housed separately.

With the three-hour boat ride behind me, I was ready to get up and move. After a quick coffee to reheat my boiler room, I was introduced to Michelle Staaf, a spirited young woman and one of the three guides in camp. In remote locations, where tragic consequences are but a misstep away, qualified leadership is crucial, and it was clear these were professionals, all having attended the same guide school in Sweden. The fact they were half my age inspired confidence rather than concern.

I spent that first evening casting flies to Arctic char in the camp's home water, a 300-metre-long stream tumbling out of a small lake into the bay. Over an hour, I landed a half-dozen beautifully coloured char in the two- to three-pound class, all on pink or orange streamers and dries. Michelle described the fishing as slow, though I thought the pace was perfect for unwinding after a long day of travel and a great way to ease into a full week of fishing and hunting in the realm of the fabled Vikings.

The caribou hunting began in the morning, as all guided hunts do, with sighting-in our rifles. Camp manager Simon Nilsson, also the chief hunting guide, showed me the rifle I'd be using, a Merkel Helix in .308 Norma Magnum topped by a 1.5-10x42 Leica scope. I'm not much of a gear-head and normally wouldn't comment, but this combination sent two clear messages. First, it reminded me that Greenland is more closely associated with Europe than North America, despite the fact its northwest coastline is only 30 kilometres or so from Canada's Ellesmere Island. Second, it told me that the Iceland-based outfitter running the camp, Lax-Á, puts an emphasis on quality.

The world's 12th-largest country, Greenland also boasts the planet's lowest human population density, so you'd think there would be plenty of space for caribou to roam. When you consider the giant island is 80 percent glacier averaging more than a kilometre and a half thick, however, it's little wonder the caribou habitat is restricted to the ice-free coastlines and innumerable islands. The hunting strategy, therefore, is to motor along, slowing down to glass each island. On one island we passed the remnants of an abandoned Greenlandic Inuit community, a stark reminder of how difficult it must be to eke out an existence in this unvarnished land.

Having spotted a dozen caribou in the scrub bush of a rather large island, we pulled in to see if there was a decent bull in the mix. Given the remoteness and the lack of hunting pressure or natural predators, I was surprised at how nervous the animals were. Before we even showed our faces, they sensed something was amiss and trotted off with their noses into the wind. For 90 minutes we pursued them but couldn't catch up, so we headed back to the boat to resume our search.

For those interested in such matters, the taxonomy of Greenland's caribou is more than a little sketchy. While there are native barren-ground caribou found in some parts of the country, there are also introduced herds from Norway's semi-domesticated reindeer population in the mix. Frankly, the ancestry of the animals we were hunting mattered little to me; I wasn't planning to qualify one for the record books. As far as I was concerned, a caribou hunt is a caribou hunt, as long as it involves fair chase.

My hunting companion, and first up for a chance at an animal, was Yuri, a Moscow businessman and avid hunter. Quiet though affable, Yuri spoke English with the stereotypical thick accent of every bad guy in a James Bond movie, but he soon proved to be a gentleman and a great hunting comrade. He got his caribou that first afternoon, a fine bull that we stalked to within 80 metres after scrambling up a cliff that hid our approach. After loading Yuri's bull into the boat, we pressed on.

Motoring around an island, we heard their explosive exhaling before we noticed two feeding humpback whales, another indication of how cold and remote this country is. Taking advantage of the viewing opportunity, we bobbed on the waves of the North Atlantic for nearly an hour, agog at the close-up spectacle of some of the world's largest, though seldom seen, creatures.

Back at camp after our amazing first outing, I listened to stories of a 100-fish day from the angling guests, dined on Arctic char and ended my day on the lodge deck, watching the northern lights run wild in shimmers and streaks of emerald.

The following morning, it was my turn to tag out. We were glassing only our third island when we spotted a group of 15 animals, including what looked like three decent bulls.

Immediately, we motored to the backside of the rocky island, beached and planned our approach.

After climbing to the highest point between the boat and where we believed the caribou were headed, we slowly crawled up to the edge of the precipice. Peering carefully over the top, we saw two bulls and two cows feeding undisturbed 100 metres below us. We had no idea where the other 11 caribou had gone, but one of the bulls below was a good one, adorned with numerous top points and one shovel.

With the wind in our favour, I had plenty of time to settle in and shoot. As the bull dropped, and before the sound of the shot had dissipated, the rest of the herd exploded into view. They'd been so tight to the rock face directly below us that we hadn't been able to see them.

On the cruise back to camp, I asked Simon to pull up to a 15-metre-tall iceberg so I could chip off some slabs of what may well have been 15,000-year-old ice. That evening, watching a repeat performance from *Aurora borealis*, I reflected on the day's hunt and sipped my scotch, chilled Greenland style.

I fished the next two days. Near the outlet of one stream, the brilliantly hued char had congregated en masse, eager to move into their spawning water. I literally caught a fish with nearly every cast. To cap off the angling day, a few of us went cod jigging, landing a half-dozen fish weighing up to 12 pounds; they were a great hit around the dinner table that evening.

On the boat ride back to Narsarsuaq Airport, we stopped at the site of Eric the Red's initial settlement, circa 984 AD. The Vikings disappeared from Greenland in the late 1400s, though no one is quite sure why. Perhaps they'd learned something about the country that just didn't fit their lifestyle. As for me? Greenland suited me just fine, and I would have stayed longer, but I had a plane to catch to neighbouring Iceland and three days of fly-fishing for Atlantic salmon.

∽

In stark contrast to Greenland's rugged and uninviting landscape, Iceland struck me as an enchanting land of refinement. The capital, Reykjavik, and the many towns through which we passed were modern, clean and quaint, while the countryside was a dichotomy of rolling green pastures and impassable lava deserts. What few wooded areas I saw were stunted by Canadian standards, and I was advised that if I got lost in one of these forests, all I had to do was stand up.

Travelling with me was Jóhann Ólafsson, Lax-Á's director of marketing. It's been said that Atlantics are the proverbial fish of a thousand casts, but Jóhann was determined to prove that simply wasn't the case in Iceland. Our first stop was East Ranga River Lodge, a full-service destination that brought to mind the traditional European salmon fishing I've read about. It was first class all the way, from the individual gillies for each guest to the heated wader room and the five-star dining.

Unfortunately, the water was unseasonably high and cold, and the wind was up, so fishing was challenging and slow. Benefiting from his expertise with a 15-foot two-handed fly rod, Jóhann did manage to hook and land a small female on the second morning. While I had hits on two successive casts without a hook-up, all I got for my efforts was a hook buried deep in my finger that took the two of us 15 minutes, and no small amount of blood, to extract.

That afternoon, we drove four hours to Iceland's north shore (apparently, you can drive around the entire island nation in a day or less). Our destination was the picturesque Svartá River, often referred to as Iceland's best-kept secret when it comes to salmon streams. Much of the upper section we'd be fishing was only 10 to 20 metres wide, making it considerably more accessible than the East Ranga for a one-handed caster such as myself.

As with all of Iceland's rivers, the Svartá is divided into carefully managed named sections, or beats. Rod days are restricted and monitored, so Jóhann and I shared just one rod, meaning we couldn't be in the water at the same time. That suited me just fine, as I'm much more comfortable fishing with another angler rather than under a guide's constant direction. That's not to say I didn't welcome any advice from Jóhann, who has all the characteristics of an excellent guide. And most importantly, he really wanted me to catch fish.

As quickly as we could get unpacked we were in the water, having opted for the do-it-yourself cabin rather than the full-service lodge, meaning we could fish, eat and sleep on our own schedule. My spirits were buoyed when I hooked and successfully fought a beautiful chrome salmon in the first hour, but then dampened somewhat when the hook popped as I was attempting to beach the fish. Nonetheless, there's nothing like fighting that first salmon to give you the confidence that there are more fish in the river…and that they can be enticed to bite.

The next morning, we awoke to clear and calm weather, a harbinger of what was to become the kind of day salmon anglers dream about. On only my sixth down-and-across cast, I hooked and landed a 25½-inch bright chrome hen that repeatedly cartwheeled across the pool before eventually succumbing. In the next pool, I caught another silver beauty, this time a 27½-incher with a prominent kype.

Throughout the day, we continued to catch fish, some fighting in aerial combat mode, while others were more subdued but no less ferocious. My last fish was the biggest of the day, a hard-fighting male that I fooled with a #14 Collie Dog tube fly. By the time we had to reel in and call it a day, we'd landed nine salmon and lost a few more. Fish of a thousand casts? As Jóhann had contended, not in Iceland.

Especially when the Norse gods of fishing are on your side.

—ww—

24

THE NAMIBIAN MACNAB

Namibia is one of the last places that comes to mind when thinking about catching fish. A country best known for its great deserts, the Kalahari and the Namib, it doesn't exactly scream angling. Still, I was keen to give it a go. I've always been an optimist, and fortunately, I suspect that Danene van der Westhuyzen must be one as well.

Danene and her husband, Gysbert, own and operate Aru Game Lodges, a hunting safari operator in Namibia. When I suggested to her that I wanted to pursue a Macnab challenge, she was immediately on board. A Macnab challenge? And what does it have to do with hunting, let alone catching fish?

It all dates back to the 1925 novel, *John Macnab*, by Scottish writer, historian and politician John Buchan, who between 1935 and 1940 served as Canada's 15th Governor General. The book centres on the exploits of three bored members of London's upper crust seeking a little excitement.

Using the collective cover name of "John Macnab," they send letters to three prominent Scottish landowners, warning them that they intend to poach two stags and a salmon from their estates. They sweeten the deal by offering to donate £100 to charity if they get caught. If they succeed, however, the landowners must donate £50 instead. Each of the challenges is accepted, and the game is on.

Today, the Macnab challenge is still alive, although poaching is no longer a part of it, replaced instead by fair chase. The challenge is quite popular in Great Britain, where there are several variations of the specific species involved. For example, the "Classic Macnab" now includes a stag, a salmon and a brace of grouse, prized quarry in the Scottish Highlands.

Recently, the challenge has gained a following in southern Africa. There, the Macnab requires that an individual shoot a big-game animal, a brace of game birds and land a fish all in one day, again employing fair-chase tactics. Having hunted in Africa on several occasions, I've taken many of the big-game animals that interest me and can withstand the scrutiny of my banker. So on this trip, I was keen to hunt birds as well as big game, and that led to the notion of pursuing southern Africa's version of the Macnab.

And yes, that also demanded catching a fish in the largely desert nation of Namibia.

As a prelude to taking the challenge, I first enjoyed five days of hunting with professional hunter, Stephan Joubert, taking an eland, a kudu and a steenbok, along with a wide assortment of upland game birds. Stephan, in his mid-20s, was born in South Africa and raised in England before moving to Namibia in 2012 to begin his career as a PH. An avid wingshooter who worked through his teens at a British shooting club, Stephan was the ideal candidate to guide me to a Macnab.

As we got to know each other, he revealed his growing excitement about the challenge. In fact, as I was to discover, he'd been texting pals in England about the opportunity to guide a colonial in the effort.

We were up early on Macnab day. Our plan required that we have our big-game animal and birds in the bag before 10:00 AM, as we had a three-hour trip to the nearest legitimate fish-holding water. Fellow PH Pedri Enslin joined us, and by 6:30 AM we were on the road with Pedri at the wheel of the Land Cruiser and Stephan gauging the wind and making last-minute tactical decisions.

I was just happy to be along for the ride. Hell, I was on a vacation of sorts and had nothing to lose if we weren't successful. And in the spirit of *John Macnab*'s three fictional British members of the upper class, I was simply looking for an interesting and exciting challenge. For Stephan and Pedri, however, my challenge had become a matter of professional pride.

Twenty minutes later, Stephan and I walked into the wind in search of a trophy springbok, the quintessential gazelle species of southern Africa's arid open grass- and scrublands. They remind me of pronghorn antelope in their size, colouration and habitat preferences, and they're equally wary of danger, springing away at the first hint of peril. With some 6000 springbok on the vast ranch we were hunting, and given the number I'd seen each day, I expected this to be the least challenging component of my Macnab. But nearly three kilometres of walking later, with no springbok in sight, I was beginning to second-guess myself. Stephan was getting downright edgy. Just as we were reconsidering our strategy, however, Stephan set up the sticks.

Shooting sticks are core to the hunting experience across what explorer and journalist Henry Stanley (he of "Dr. Livingstone, I presume" fame) once called the "Dark Continent." PHs use them as walking sticks, as pokers to prod at spoor and push thornbush aside and as pointers when describing landscape features. When they're planted upright in the ground, however, the message is clear: it's shooting time.

Quick as a cobra, I had my .30-06 nestled in the forks and the crosshairs centred on the dandy springbok ram that had stepped out from behind an acacia tree some 125 metres away. Or so I thought I had the crosshairs centred. I squeezed the trigger, and unfortunately, the springbok did what springbok do when alarmed, disappearing in a flash with its distinctive gait. It was a clean miss, right over the ram's back.

Nobody says much after a missed shot. I was feeling a mixture of disappointment, dejection and embarrassment because it was a shot I should have made. Stephan was clearly discouraged, too. Even within the context of the Macnab challenge, he didn't want to settle for anything less than a quality ram, and that's what I'd just missed. Saying little else, he radioed Pedri to bring the truck. We were going to have to try elsewhere.

We'd only walked 100 metres; however, when we simultaneously spotted another ram. It's amazing how such apparently open cover can conceal so many animals. This ram was farther out, nearly 200 metres and quartered away—definitely not a "gimme," considering springbok are small animals and I was shooting off sticks. Fortunately, at the shot, the ram fell in his tracks, and both Stephan and I felt palpable relief. And with Pedri already on the way with the truck, we hadn't lost much time. It was 7:22 AM. Next up, a brace of birds.

Sandgrouse are as closely related to pigeons as they are to grouse, resembling a cross between the two. They have a head much like a pigeon's, and they fly like a pigeon, but their cryptic plumage reminds one instantly of a grouse. They water each morning with the precision of a German train schedule, so Stephan, Pedri and I bounced across the veld to a waterhole where we'd already enjoyed success a couple of mornings earlier.

Sandgrouse aren't the only game birds to visit that waterhole, and we hadn't been there long when a small flight of doves spirited in. I swung on the lead bird, and it tumbled onto the sand, but missed with my second shot as the remaining birds clawed skyward. Then all went quiet, with the silence making the passing minutes agonizingly painful.

Finally, another small flock of doves cascaded down, and I cleanly picked a bird from the bunch. We had our brace, as per Macnab rules, but we'd decided earlier that sandgrouse would be our bird of choice as they're much more revered in the wingshooting world. Still, if all else failed, the doves would serve as a legitimate back-up.

"Sandgrouse," Stephan whispered, "10 o'clock." And sure enough, a dozen of them were headed our way. With my first shot, I cleanly dropped a bird but came up empty with the second barrel. Not to worry, I thought, as more were sure to arrive. But as with the springbok, our prey wasn't following the script, and the minutes ticked away with only the occasional flight of doves dropping in.

Eventually, the telltale call of sandgrouse met our ears, and we turned to the eastern sky, watching eight small specks grow as they closed in. I'm not sure if I was anxious or feeling the pressure, but I fired both barrels with not a feather to show for the effort. Stephan, in his eminently positive manner, brushed it off, while Pedri muttered some good-natured jibe about my shooting prowess. I just squeezed the smoothbore a little tighter.

When another flight swung through with equally fruitless results, the pressure continued to mount. A fourth flock followed soon after, and I can't really say whether I picked an individual bird or just swung on the flock. Whatever the case, at the report a sandgrouse folded, and before it had even hit the ground I hollered, "Let's go fishing, boys!"

After photographing the springbok and the birds, we raced back to the lodge where Stephan and Pedri had earlier loaded another truck with fishing gear and grub. By 9:30 AM we were back on the road, ahead of schedule.

Our destination was Namibia's largest reservoir, the 25-square-kilometre Hardap Dam, on the aptly named Fish River in the Hardap Game Reserve. It was a two-and-a-half hour drive, most of it gravel, to the park gate, where we secured fishing licenses from the attendant. We then drove partway around the reservoir and pulled down to the water's edge.

We wouldn't be seeking fish nearly as refined as the Atlantic salmon of Buchan's Scottish estates. Hardap Dam is populated with what I'd best describe as rough fish, an assortment of catfish, carp, yellowfish, barbels and other similar Namibian species endemic to warm, freshwater lakes and rivers.

Our presentation wasn't anything nearly as snooty as a gently cast dry fly. Instead, we mushed corn together with a fetid meal attractant and squished the resulting glop onto a small hook suspended below a lead weight. Then all we had to do was heave the works out as far as possible, hoping the bait didn't fly off in the process, then place the rod into a holder and park our butts on the shoreline to wait.

We'd only been there about 20 minutes when Pedri's line twitched. He grabbed the pole, set the hook and reeled in a largemouth yellowfish weighing a couple of pounds. It would have been easy enough for Pedri to hand me his rod, let me reel in the fish and proclaim our Macnab a success. But true to the spirit of our adventure, we'd all agreed that it would only count if I landed a fish on a line that I'd baited and cast. So on we fished.

Fortunately, the wait wasn't long before my rod tip also nodded. The boys cheered as I set the hook and carefully reeled another yellowfish in to shore. As I dragged the wriggling mass up on to the beach, we had high-fives all around. We'd met the challenge and had our Macnab! Pedri cracked open some cold ones while Stephan texted the news to his friends abroad.

Stephan and Pedri suggested that ours may have been the first-ever Macnab recorded in Namibia. I suspect it's probably been accomplished in the country's extreme north along the famed Caprivi Strip, where the Zambezi River offers plenty of opportunity for the revered tiger fish. But our Macnab may well have been the first in the heart of Namibia.

In any case, I was proud to have accepted the challenge...and succeeded. Some might suggest we were crazy to give it a go in central Namibia. I believe it would have been crazy *not* to try. And I can't help but think that John Buchan, nearly a century after creating the very idea of the Macnab challenge, is smiling from beyond the grave, knowing it lives on.

Even in a desert.

—ɯ—

KEN BAILEY

Born in Nottingham, England, the son of a Canadian Air Force pilot, Ken was an Air Force "brat," and as a result lived in several towns, cities and provinces across Canada while growing up. Angling and hunting have been lifelong passions and hobbies for Ken, who has fished and/or hunted in Africa, South America, Central America and Europe as well as across much of North America.

A 40-year career in wildlife and the publishing industry afforded Ken the opportunity to pursue his passion for the outdoors, and led to many professional opportunities. He has written more than 1000 published magazine articles and columns since 1989, contributing to *Outdoor Canada, Alberta Outdoorsmen, Wildfowl, Whitetails Unlimited, African Hunting Gazette, Outdoor Life, Delta Waterfowl, Outdoor Edge, Canadian Sportfishing, National Post, Conservation, Varmint Magazine, Canadian Firearms Journal, Alberta Fishing Guide,* and *The Angler's Post,* among others.

Ken is one of those people who likes to try everything, and over the years has been a certified sport parachutist and a certified scuba diver. He has visited the North Magnetic Pole and has hiked and paddled many of Canada's great trails and rivers.

Married with two sons, he and his artist wife like to travel, although by most accounts they are both homebodies who enjoy curling up at home with a movie or a good book such as his current offering of *No Place Like Home,* where he recounts his many adventures fishing and hunting across Canada.